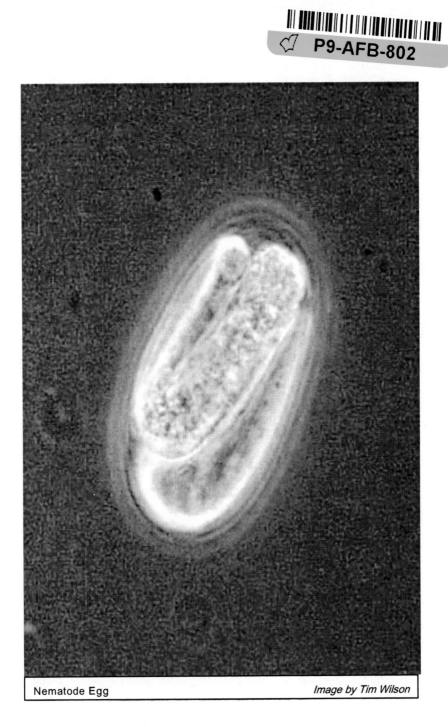

Nematode Egg

Image by Tim Wilson

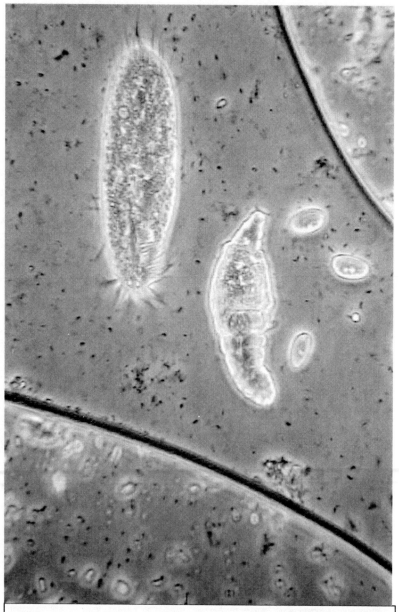

Rotifer with Large & Small Ciliates   *Image by Tim Wilson*

Compost Tea Making

by
Marc Remillard

Ascension Press

~~~~~~~Table of Contents~~~~~~~

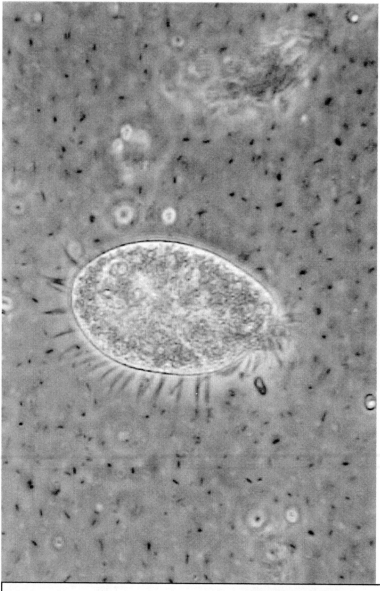

Protozoa-Ciliate 250X · *Image by Tim Wilson*

What Is Compost Tea?

The chemistry may be complex, but the concept is simple. Compost is placed into a bucket of water, and air is pumped into the bottom of the bucket, percolating up through the tea and soil. Aerobic bacteria, protozoa, and fungi grow and flourish in the presence of all of the oxygen. Compost tea is a brewed water extract of compost in which beneficial microbes and fungi are encouraged to multiply.

Using compost tea is like using compost multiplied by 100. One of the great things about compost tea is how *little* compost it takes to make a large batch of tea!

Compost tea is concentrated, and is often diluted with water prior to application. It can be used for either a root fertilizer or a foliar spray. The benefits of compost tea on the roots and leaves of plants are many, and will be discussed later. It's enough to say that compost tea *greatly* improves the health of plants.

Compost tea has no strong odor, only a faint pleasing earthy smell, so it can be used for your inside plants as well as outside. Therefore, it may be brewed indoors as well as outdoors.

What is described in this text in detail is a *method* for the creation of compost tea. While many roads may lead to Rome, this method is by far the most commonly used, being that it is easy, safe, reliable, inexpensive, and extremely effective.

These techniques involve the culturing and preening of beneficial aerobic (oxygen loving) microbes, while in turn discouraging the growth of anaerobic (oxygen avoiding) organisms. That theme runs throughout this treatise, until the final chapter, when we will add an interesting twist by suggesting the introduction of some specific beneficial anaerobes to enhance our already powerful aerobic compost tea blends.

The widespread use of compost tea is inevitable, as it is easy to make, and the single most powerful tool any type of horticulturist can have in their arsenal, whether they be a commercial grower or a backyard gardener.

Compost tea is a microbial concentrate loaded with beneficial bacteria and fungi. When that huge microbial population is turned loose into your garden, orchard, vineyard or lawn, you are effectively re-introducing beneficial healthy life forms into your environment. These are some of the very same types of organisms that should have been there in the first place. Your plants will immediately respond favorably, as they will be receiving the nutrients they need *naturally* as a result of the microbes being there.

The plants initial positive response is only the beginning of a dramatic uptrend in their overall health. Eventually, not only will they be getting more (and more complex) nutrients, but the soil in the root zone will better retain moisture, have increased aeration, and the roots will be more protected from predation. The roots of any plant will therefore grow considerably larger.

Likewise, in the leaf zone the foliage will receive more nutri-ents and be better protected from diseases and pests.

Here is an analogy of conventional agriculture. Imagine plants growing in soil with no life in it, waiting for their next shot of fertilizer. The plants are in prison, receiving food adequate for their survival, but not for any quality of life. They live in a sterile hell, producing fruit because they love to do so. However, the fruit is tasteless, and the plants are weak and anemic, rendering them prone to attack from the barbarian hordes—diseases and insects.

In a healthy agricultural environment, plants and beneficial microbes have various complex symbiotic relationships. *They* consider pests and diseases to be vulgar and uncivilized, and send volunteers out to attack and neutralize them.

By harnessing the power of the microbial world for the benefit of your plants and yourself, your environment can be much healthier—naturally.

Imagine, your empire could be huge, with billions of workers willing to tirelessly maintain it—for free!

The reader is encouraged to read the entire book. We have included a bit of soft science, with some technical terminology-much of which may not be important to remember. What *is* important is to grasp the general idea of it, which the science will eloquently help in the understanding and nature of compost tea.

Please share your experiences in our forum at:

compostteamaking.com

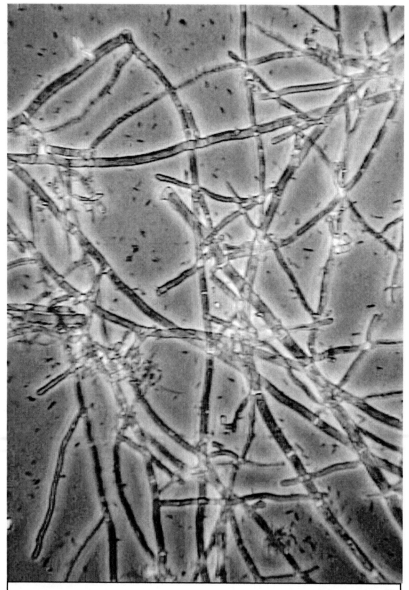

Fungal Hyphae   *Image by Tim Wilson*

Introduction

My first encounter with compost tea was somewhat of a revelation. It was a sensory experience, quite subjective, but I found myself using one of the most important practical tools of the scientist—*observation*.

I have developed my own novel, simple way to grow tomatoes in containers on a concrete patio. The tomato plants are encouraged to grow unsupported—out of the containers—onto the patio. The branches are arranged radially growing outwards from the center, and then supported by flower pots to keep them off of the patio, with the tomatoes not quite touching the concrete. The reflection off of the concrete in the day, and the gentle warmth radiating from it at night help ripen the fruit quite nicely in the northern latitude where I live.

The patio is the area where I take my summer evening repose, so by default the tomatoes tend to receive plenty of casual attention.

After doing the R&D on the design of a compost tea brewer for a company, I took the prototype home for testing. I made my first five gallon batch of compost tea the day after I'd planted seven 8" tomato starts in containers. The varietal was Japanese Black Trifele, a hardy but tasty heirloom tomato. Needless to say, the new tomato starts got drenched with my first batch of diluted compost tea.

Three days later, barefoot on the warm, wet patio, I found myself staring at those plants, almost dumbfounded. It was not just the fact that the plants had obviously grown larger, and not suffered any typical transplanting shock, it was the color that caught my attention. It was green beyond green, bordering on luminescence. I may consider myself to be an above average gardener, but I had *never* seen tomato plants look like that. I actually fancied that I may have been seeing a bit of their auric field. Now I must confess to have been sporting a glass of red wine, however recently poured, but if anything the wine should have dulled those finer senses.

The bottom line is though; I just kept standing there with my mouth open staring at that intense vibrant green. In that one long wonderful moment I converted, became a believer—a card carrying devotee of compost tea.

My tomato plants were only a minor part of the total amount of biomass of foliage under cultivation on that patio. Typically, I am the vegetable guy while my wife is the flower deva. That first batch of tea also ended up gracing her flowers, which began growing so rapidly, and producing such gorgeous colors that it initiated a buying frenzy on her part, including varieties she had not previously had success with. Eventually, our humble back patio was transformed into a veritable hanging garden of Babylon. The results were truly amazing.

If I were King, I would simply have the heralds proclaim a decree:

Every gardener and plant lover
Must make and use compost tea
And you *will* enjoy it!

But alas, being a mere commoner, I spread the good word, and became a spokesman *for*, the televangelist *of* compost tea.

My plants have been healed!

After speaking with many gardeners, I realized that the majority were aware of compost tea, but knew very little about it. The off-the-shelf "compost tea" products are questionable at best, and not in the same league as our fresh-brewed teas. As we shall see, true aerobic compost tea has no real shelf life, and should be used within the first few hours after completing the brewing process.

The few gardeners I spoke with that were making it were mostly using methods I considered inadequate, resulting in teas that probably had low populations of beneficial microbes, which as we shall also learn, may not sufficiently discourage disease-causing anaerobic organisms. We need to infuse plenty of oxygen into our compost tea brews.

One of these old techniques is known as the "stick method," which entails simply stirring a container of compost in water several times per day, or pouring it back & forth from bucket to bucket a few times. Serviceable teas have certainly been made in this way, but it really depends on how often it was stirred, how vigorously, and what nutrients, if any, were added.

The stick method dates back at least as far as the Roman era, when Cato discussed a form of compost tea in his book, "De Agricultura." The Romans gleaned a lot of their knowledge of agriculture and viticulture from (their enemies) the Carthaginians who, in that era were known to have developed considerable prowess in these fields. Some of the earliest successful vineyards in Spain were a direct result of Carthaginian influence. Carthage itself was originally settled by Phoenicians escaping from their homeland in present day Lebanon, which today still has some world-class wine-grape vineyards.

Using the same compost as used in the method described above, with relatively low-tech equipment, we can easily create healthy aerobic compost teas with very high populations of beneficial microbes.

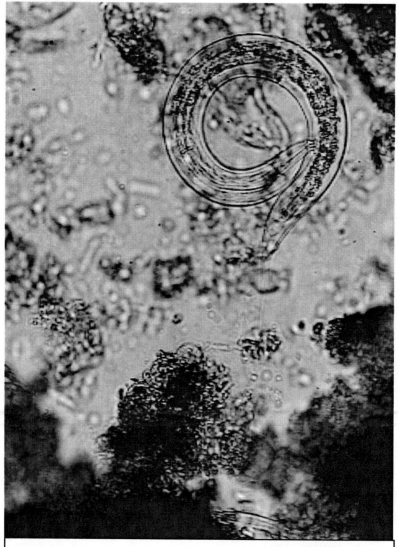

Nematode   *Image by Tim Wilson*

Understanding Compost Tea

The complexity of the microbial world is staggering, humbling for those of us comfortable considering ourselves as lords and masters of this planet. Our arrogance may be short lived, abruptly terminated when we set eye-to-microscope, to observe the fascinating and colorful realm of the tiny.

This is the domain of nematodes, protozoa, yeasts, fungi, bacteria, and minute viruses. In the microbial kingdom there is no right and wrong, no good or bad, no philosophy, religion, cruelty, or kindness. It is however, our world, even if it remains unseen, and typically ignored by us.

Our dependence on microbes cannot be understated or ignored. We manipulate and encourage microbes to help us make bread, wine, beer, cheese, yogurt, sour cream, buttermilk, miso, soy sauce, sour kraut, kimchee, vinegar, and medicines. Also, aerobic/anaerobic pairs of bacteria are used in sophisticated waste management programs to help purify water with high levels of petroleum, dyes, and toxins.

Our bodies, much like the earths soils, contain both beneficial and non-beneficial microbes. It has been said that 100 trillion microorganisms exist on and in the human body.

Microbes were first observed by Anton van Leeuwenhoek, a Dutch trader and talented lens grinder. With his unique hand held microscope, he was first able to observe cells in 1673, and finally bacteria in 1677. In a scraping of plaque from his own teeth, he observed, "many little living animalcules, very prettily a moving."

This may conjure up unsettling images, considering the lack of proper dental hygiene in 17th century Europe, but even today with daily brushing we harbor hosts of bacteria in our mouths. It's enough to say that Leeuwenhoek's portrait, showing him holding his famous little microscope does *not* depict him with a big bleached Hollywood smile.

Almost two hundred years later, in 1861, 39 year old Louis Pasteur won a prize offered by the Paris Academy of Science concerning the persistent idea that germs grew by "spontaneous generation". The theory was discreetly linked to the then predominant belief in Creationism, and held to the idea that microbes simply popped in out of thin air. Pasteur proved the idea incorrect, showing us that microbes do have reproductive capabilities, and can be introduced into a culture medium from the air as well.

In 1863, Napoleon III hired Pasteur to investigate why 25% of all French wine went bad before reaching the consumer. At the time France produced much more wine than they do today. 25% of the total production equated to millions of bottles of spoiled wine annually, resulting in a national travesty that hampered the French economy. Pasteur then produced his famous treatise "*Études sur le Vin,*" which became a cornerstone of modern microbiology. He discovered the role that oxygen plays in wine, which set the stage for understanding the differences between aerobic and anaerobic microbes. Pasteur suggested heating the finished wine to 140° F. to subdue the microbes. Unfortunately, that would not only ruin the flavor, but would also volatilize off some of the alcohols which helped protect the wine in the first place. However, the technique did work well with milk, helping to give it a longer shelf life in an era prior to refrigeration. Thus we have the simple process which still bears his name.

The common thought of a society tends to oversimplify new scientific discoveries. Eventually, western society began to view *all* bacteria and microbes as unnecessary evils.

As history shows us, the pendulum that Louis Pasteur nudged eventually swung far to one side, many years later causing baby-boomers to rebel against what they considered repulsive; that sterile, chlorinated, pseudo-Utopian vision of the early

1960's. Contrary to any rational thought, common dogma held all bacteria as a prime enemy.

While the men of the era were concerned with the rise of Communism, and the threat of the A-bomb, American housewives went on the aggressive on the microbial battlefield, and took no prisoners. Armed with dangerous (some now illegal) chemicals, they were the heavy cavalry of the clean camp.

The same philosophy also applied to agriculture, where microbes, insects, and plant diseases were lumped together as a group that were considered best eliminated. Farmers in that era remembered the "dust bowl" of the 1930's, when locusts, bole weevils, and diseases ruined entire crops and families. It is only understandable why they embraced the new methods of agriculture that were being promoted by the USDA in association with various universities. The idea was simplistic. Eliminate the pests, and feed the plants with fertilizers.

We are older and wiser now, but are faced with the monumental task of rejuvenating agricultural soils worldwide that have become weakened from the over use of pesticides, herbicides, non-organic nitrogen fertilizers, compaction, and excessive mechanical manipulation. Most agricultural soils farmed with conventional methods are microbial dead zones—a graveyard for bacteria, fungi, protozoa, and nematodes.

Why are nitrate fertilizers detrimental to microbes?

In 1928 commercial chemists came up with the technique for making inexpensive nitrogen-based fertilizers. The synthetic fertilizers do their job well, providing nutrients directly to the plants. But what has occurred because of their continual use is a vicious cycle of soil degradation in a downward spiral resulting in agricultural soils devoid of life.

The overuse of chemical fertilizers impairs plant metabolism, and accelerates the accumulation of amino acids, nitrate ions, and amides in leaves. The result is plants with a weaker resistance to diseases and insects. The plants therefore become somewhat dysfunctional, requiring even more fertilizers and pesticides as well.

Another obvious reason nitrogen-based fertilizers are detrimental to microbes and worms is because the fertilizers are salt-based. Nitrate salts to be exact. Salt is an irritant to worms and means death to many microbes.

Some fertilizers also contain herbicides and insecticides, the introduction of which hearkens the death knell for most microbes.

Environmental researchers are quick to point out that the artificial introduction of nitrogen into our environment is beginning to have serious impacts in many ecosystems. Agriculture is not the only culprit. Nitrogen is also pumped into the air by power plants and vehicle emissions.

Most nitrogen does not stay in the atmosphere the way carbon dioxide from carbon fuel does, but precipitates out within a few days. Ammonia—a mixture of hydrogen and nitrogen— becomes ammonium when mixed with water and acts like a fertilizer when it falls to the ground as rain.

While at first glance fertilizing our natural world may seem like a good idea, in reality it is not. Fertilizing native plants upsets the delicate relationships between species in many ecosystems, particularly in desert and alpine areas. Species that respond to nitrogen favorably tend to over-compete, and eventually dominate plants that are important for the symbiotic general health of the particular area.

Nitrogen from agriculture also bleeds into the water systems, which eventually flow into our oceans and lakes.

Quoting from the Christian Science Monitor:

"The most dramatic impacts can be seen in the growth of coastal dead zones where excessive nutrients in the water—fueled by runoff of fertilizers—has suffocated or driven away ocean animals. In the Gulf of Mexico, fish and shrimp have been eliminated in an 8,000 square mile dead zone

at the mouth of the Mississippi River. More than 400 dead zones with a total area of 245,000 square kilometers were identified last year (2009)."(Written prior to the 2010 BP Gulf of Mexico oil spill)

Many farmers are aware of this problem, and are paring down the per-acre volume of nitrogen fertilizer they use. It is interesting to note that crop yields have remained consistent. The general consensus is that in the past they were using more fertilizer than was necessary, the excess simply flowing out into the environment. It has been estimated that in Chinese rice growing areas, the use of nitrogen is so inefficient that as much as 75% ends up in the rivers, lakes, and oceans.

In the USA the Federal government is working to help improve the efficiency of farm nitrogen fertilizers by 25 percent.

Why are microbes important for healthy soil?

Microbes are the alchemists that break down organic matter into smaller building blocks. When we add compost tea to the soil around our plants, we are adding microbial life to the soil, which provides nutrients naturally for the plants.

In a natural environment, soils tend to contain an extremely wide range of bacteria, fungi, nematodes, and protozoa. Their populations are actually so diverse, we do not even have species names for most of them! We have learned enough however, concerning the habits and life cycles of the various microbes and fungi to begin to grasp the importance of these sometimes symbiotic, sometimes competitive organisms.

In many ways plants are not so different from humans. When we perspire, the sticky compounds on our skin are actually considered good eating for various microbes. Likewise, plants use some of the energy created from photosynthesis to "perspire" in both the root zone, or *rhizoshpere,* and in the leaf zone, or *phyllosphere.* The perspiration, or secretion is known as plant *exudates.*

The nutrients, carbohydrates, and proteins in root exudates are a basic microbial food source, fostering a veritable feeding frenzy amongst bacteria, fungi, protozoa, nematodes, arthropods, and ultimately, mammals and birds. Some of the microbes feed on the plants exudates, some on exudates given off *by* each other, while many feed *on* each other.

The majority of this microbial feast occurs within the rhizosphere, an area extending out only 2mm from the roots. The plant benefits from all of the activity around its roots by taking in nutrients produced by the exudates and the decomposition of the participants at this microbial dinner party. In fact, the plant actually controls the guest list, as to whom is invited and when they shall come to the table—all based on the needs of the plant. The plant regulates who attends by altering the nature of it's exudate secretions, kind of like playing different music to attract the appropriate guests.

The Microbial Dinner Party

Bacteria

Bacteria are the smallest, possibly most important workers in the soil building process. They increase soil structure, water-retention capacity, and create passageways for the diffusion of oxygen into, and carbon dioxide out of the soil. They also play an important role in recycling three important elements: sulfur, carbon, and nitrogen. Bacteria, by diverse ways, have the ability to retain nutrients (N, P, S, Ca, Fe, etc.) and provide those nutrients for plants, as well as serve to decompose plant-toxic materials and excess residues. Bacteria help build soils that have been damaged by compaction, over-tillage, inorganic fertilization, and toxic chemicals such as pesticides and fungicides. Bacteria are also a major food source for other, larger microbes.

In foliar compost tea applications, bacteria have a symbiotic relationship with the plants. Beneficial bacteria are applied in hordes, thereby dominating leaf surfaces, leaving no room for pathogens to grow or feed, while at the same time improving the plants intake of foliar nutrients. When microbes respire carbon dioxide, that causes the leaf stomates to open, allowing more nutrients in. In dry weather, the bacteria are less active, giving off less carbon dioxide, which causes the stomates to open less, effectively governing the plant's nutrient intake. Bacteria also hold and metabolize nutrients in various ways, many of which become available for the plants through the leaves.

In today's science, bacteria are divided into three main groups, or **Domains**.

- *Domain Archaea*

- *Domain Eukarya*

- *Domain Bacteria*

Bacteria and *Archaea* are both Prokaryotes. It is interesting to note that ribosomal RNA analysis indicates that *Archaea* are actually more closely related to *Eukarya*, the domain that contains humans. Our bodies have more in common with archaic bacteria than they do with bacteria proper.

Archaea may have been some of the first organisms on our planet. They exist in some almost unfathomable environments, such as: inside rocks, in super-heated acidic (pH 2) geyser water, extreme Antarctic cold, in acidic volcanic vents in total darkness on the bottom of the ocean floor, and environments with high salt concentrations such as the Great Salt Lake in Utah and the Dead Sea in Israel. To claim that *Archaea* are tough is a gross understatement.

Our focus however, is primarily concerned with organisms associated with the earth's soils and plants, *Bacteria* being the most important.

Every bacterium has a necessary place in our world, have their own job to do, but not all are beneficial for the health of

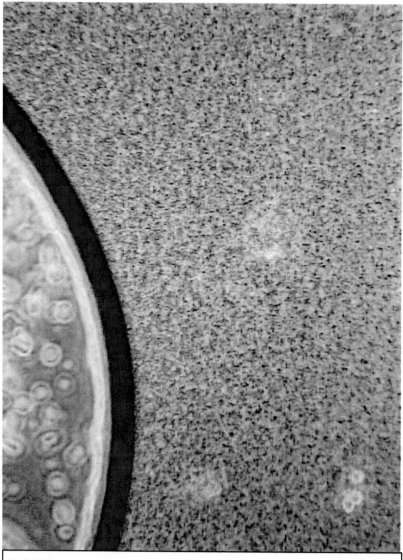

| Air Bubble and Bacteria | *Image by Tim Wilson* |

The tiny dots on the right are bacteria. Notice how there are a higher concentration of them near the air bubble.

soil, plants, or inevitably, ourselves. Undesirable bacteria are usually anaerobic, and are considered to be **pathogens.** Our goal in the creation of compost tea is to discourage the growth of pathogens, while encouraging the population of beneficial aerobic bacteria.

Anaerobic bacteria have important roles to play in our natural environment, and are identified by their notorious tendency to flourish in low-oxygen environments—a truly remarkable characteristic. Anaerobic bacteria are *autotrophs*. They actually do need oxygen, but glean it from chemically bound up forms. They get it indirectly, by "breathing" CO_2, NO_3, NO_2, and SO_4 etc. We can observe how oxygen is present in each of the compounds listed above. We used the term "breathing" very loosely, as anaerobic bacteria actually have very diverse ways they use to metabolize the oxygen.

In a compost pile or in a compost tea, the presence of anaerobic bacteria can generally be identified by foul smells. For the purposes of this text, we are discouraging the growth of anaerobes in our teas.

Aerobic bacteria are oxygen-loving organisms that tend to be more delicate than, and may be dominated by anaerobic bacteria—given a lack of oxygen. However, in the correct environment aerobics will easily dominate anaerobic populations.

In the making of compost teas, we are simply choosing to culture aerobic organisms because they perform functions favorable to our cause. Our goal is to provide first class conditions for aerobic organisms to grow and flourish.

Fungi

In 1885, German scientist Albert Bernard Frank discovered that pine seedlings grew better in sterile soil inoculated with forest fungi than in plain sterile soil. He realized that the trees actually benefit from the presence of fungus in the root zone.

Today, the symbiotic relationships between plant roots and fungi is termed "mycorrhizae". The presence of mycorrhizal fungi in our soils is paramount, as at least 90% of all plants form mycorrhizae. Much like the unnamed bacteria, Taxonomy does not have names for most of the fungi present in soil. Thousands of species exist in only one batch of compost tea.

The importance of beneficial fungi in soil structure also cannot be understated. Many of the roles fungi have in the development of high quality soils are similar to the roles played by beneficial bacteria.

Fungi help build aggregate soil structure, and create passageways for nutrients to move through, oxygen to flow *into*, and carbon dioxide to flow out *of*. Fungi are also some of the best workers we have to combat soil compaction because of their ability to continually break up the soil. They also have their own unique, powerful ways to decompose plant residue, plant toxic materials, and decaying microbes. Fungi also retain nutrients in the fungal biomass—particularly calcium.

Fungi commonly feed on more complex sugars, and food more difficult to digest than bacteria do. Bacteria, being opportunists, are very adept at snatching up the simple sugars, leaving the remaining food for the fungi. Therefore, fungi have developed many diverse, ingenious methods for finding, securing and digesting their food.

One remarkable characteristic of fungi is their *hyphae*, which may be roughly described as arms, or branches that are sent out by the organism, extending sometimes several meters through the soil. While bacteria usually spend their lives in a small space, fungi have an extremely large sphere of influence compared to the size of their base, which for soil fungi is only several times larger than bacteria. The hyphae reach through the soil in search for food, growing at the tip. This extremely complex process is called *apical growth,* characterized by a dark spot on the growing tip.

While new cells are being pushed into the growing tip and supplied by the cytoplasm, the organism constantly exudes acidic enzymes capable of dissolving tough lignins and cellulose, then converting them into simple sugars and amino acids—food that is absorbed by the hyphae.

Some fungi can be carnivorous feeders. When the tip of a hyphae finds a nematode it spears it, allowing the nutrients from the prey to flow into the fungal organism. Another fungal species captures a nematode by lassoing it, wrapping its hyphae around the worm and strangling it, all after the fungi has released a chemical lure that attracted the nematode to it in the first place.

While these sinister dramas may sound like appropriate fodder for nightmares or a low budget horror film (*The Attack of the Killer Fungus—1956*), they are actually even more frightening considering that fungal hyphae can grow as fast as 40 micrometers per minute!

Like bacteria, fungi may feed on plant exudates, but also have been observed feeding on organisms as large as microarthropods, some of which can be seen with the naked eye.

What mycorrhizal fungi contribute in their symbiotic relationships with plants is far too vast to be covered here. However, one of the obvious gifts fungi contribute is their unique capability to liberate and transport chemically locked up minerals to the plant. The most important mineral involved in this exchange is phosphorus, but fungi also help provide calcium, copper, magnesium, iron, and zinc in available forms that plants can use.

After a foliar application of compost tea, fungi may occupy only up to 25% of the leaf surfaces, but like bacteria, their presence tends to fend off undesirables, consuming plant exudates that disease causing organisms would otherwise use for food.

In brief, mycorrhizal fungi not only act as sentries, or watch-dogs, attacking and feeding on parasites, but also provide essential nutrients that the plants would otherwise have difficulty getting.

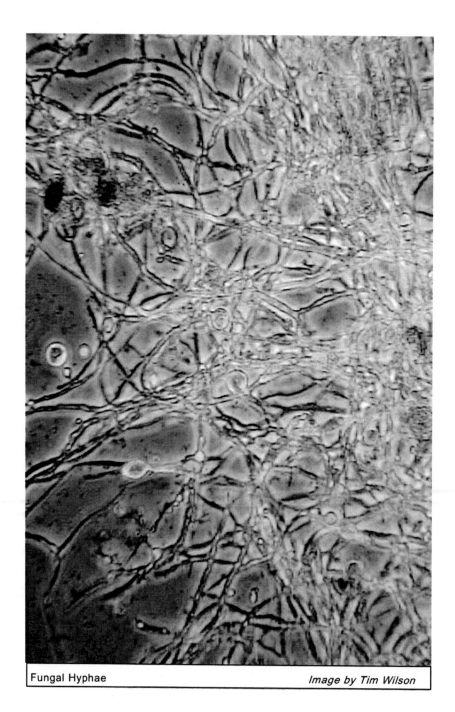

Fungal Hyphae   *Image by Tim Wilson*

Non beneficial fungi

Not all fungi are made in heaven, as all gardeners know. We must reiterate that there is no right and wrong in the microbial world.

A vivid dichotomy would be to describe our relationship with *Botrytis cinerea* (gray mold fungus). For most of us, gray mold is an unwelcome guest, a scourge in our gardens, covering and quickly rotting our strawberries and grapes. However, in southwest France *Botrytis cinerea* is welcome and encouraged to flourish in some Sauvignon Blanc and Semillon vineyards, where silky yellow -amber colored nectar is produced from totally molded clusters of grapes in the famous appellations (areas) of Sauternes, Cadillac, and Armailhac.

One of the most common commercial uses of compost tea is in wine grape vineyards, where fungal dominated teas are used in foliar applications to combat powdery mildew, downy mildew, *Botrytis cinerea,* and other diseases on red (and most white) grapes.

A healthy plant attracts the fungal and bacterial species that are good for it at the appropriate times. In turn, those beneficial organisms protect their turf, by repelling organisms that may be harmful to the plant.

However, there are times when environmental conditions and pressure from diseases become extreme and we are faced with the necessity of having to use applied products to stave off plant diseases and non-beneficial fungus. Oftentimes this may be due to our tendency to grow plants away from their native environments. Hopefully at these times we choose to be careful and discreet in our applications of sulfur, copper, and other products. What is really damaging to fungal populations are the typical evils: herbicides, fungicides, inorganic fertilizers, compaction, tillage, and, we must add—double digging, which breaks up the fungal hyphae. Soil that has been tilled too often tends to have low fungal biomass, because the fungi strands become broken up by the tiller, disk, or shovel.

Protozoa

There are over 60,000 identified types of protozoa, ranging from 5-500 microns in size. Most feed on bacteria, but some will eat fungus or even other protozoa. A hungry protozoa may eat up to 10,000 bacteria per day, so they tend to migrate to where the bacterial populations are high.

Protozoa need water to live, but may survive many years in drought conditions by encasing themselves in a cyst and going into a dormant state.

The waste produced by protozoa in the root zone is actually responsible for providing up to 80% of the nitrogen needed by plants.

However, not all types of protozoa are welcome at our plant's prestigious dinner parties, some being uncouth characters who prefer to feed on the roots of plants. A wise, healthy plant employs cannibalistic protozoa as "bouncers" who eagerly consume their unruly root-eating cousins.

A fully completed thermal compost pile needs to go into an undisturbed rest stage, cooling to below 125° (50°C) for at least one week to allow the protozoa to multiply.

Nematodes

Nematodes are essentially tiny worms that vary in size, but are typically about 0.5 millimeter in length. Scientists speculate that there may be as many a one million species of nematodes, which vary so greatly in their habits and feeding preferences that they have become the focus of volumes of studies.

We may think of nematodes as pond dwellers, but most actually live in soil. Depending on the species, they feed on bacteria, fungi, or other nematodes. Most are beneficial for soil health and plant growth, but like the unruly, root eating protozoa, some nematodes with particularly bad manners are not welcome at the party. In a healthy root zone miscreants such as these become food for predators large and small.

Compost needs to be fully composted and allowed to rest for two weeks below 115° F. (45°C) to ensure an adequate population of nematodes for the soil.

Aerobic vs. Anaerobic

Why are aerobic compost teas the safest type? Compost tea is a general term that has been used loosely to describe different types of brewed and non-brewed products. Specifically, some of the different forms of compost tea are:

- **Aerated aerobic compost tea**
- Non-aerated compost tea
- Anaerobic compost tea
- Manure tea
- Compost extract
- Compost leachate
- Fermented plant tea

All of the compost tea styles listed above are worthy of further studies, but in this text we are concerned with only one type—**Aerated aerobic compost tea**

Aerated compost tea is the style that most gardeners, horticulturists, arborists, and viticulturists will find the most useful. Other styles should be considered experimental at best. Why? **Generally** speaking, aerobic or oxygen-loving organisms create healthy compost teas, while anaerobic organisms tend to make brews not beneficial for plant growth, and may contain human pathogens.

Aerated aerobic compost teas are made by pumping air into a container of water that has good compost and specific nutrients added to it. This creates a favorable environment for beneficial microbes and fungi to reproduce and multiply in. When the brewing is completed, the amber colored compost tea contains literally billions of aerobic microbes, such as:

- Aerobic bacteria
- Aerobic fungi
- Beneficial protozoa

There may be as many as 500,000 *species* of beneficial microbes and fungi in one gram of compost tea. The same tea may contain as many as one billion beneficial aerobic bacteria per milliliter, not to mention meters of fungal hyphae, thousands of protozoa, and dozens of nematodes. Wow!

We can now begin to understand why the utilization of compost teas in our agricultural environment is of such great importance. By introducing high populations of beneficial microbes into our environment we are helping to improve both the long term general health of the soil, and the more immediate vitality of our plants.

Researchers and practitioners are learning more about the benefits of compost teas every day. Considering the sheer daunting numbers of individual microbes present in compost tea, and their complex relationships with both the environment and each other, it is apparent that what we have learned so far is really just the tip of the iceberg.

Pathogens

Escherichia coli has received plenty of attention in the press because of instances of tainted meat and other food products in the USA. Of the many sub-species of *E.coli*, the only one that is truly a human pathogen is *E.coli 0157*. Consumption of *E.coli 0157* by people with weak or immature immune systems can result in death. Many other sub-species of *E.coli* are regularly present in the environment, in our bodies, and on our unwashed hands. Some *E. coli* subspecies benefit digestion in our intestinal tracts. *E. coli*, like most true human pathogens, grow in anaerobic conditions, which are conditions with low oxygen levels. However, *E. coli* are known as *faculative* anaerobes, that thrive in anaerobic conditions but can survive in aerobic environments.

Commercial producers of compost teas may send samples of their compost or compost teas to laboratories that specialize in identifying pathogens. The presence of *E.coli* in a lab test of a compost or a compost tea is an indicator that much more dangerous anaerobic human pathogens may be present, such as: *Shigella, Salmonella, Pasteurella, Streptococci, Clostridium species, etc.*.

Please beware of the tendency to be complacent, or lazy, and think that everything will be OK just because your compost pile has all-natural organic materials in it. Organic chemistry can be really scary. You should avoid the breathing of, and skin contact with stinky, anaerobic compost, not to mention the consumption of food associated with it. Human pathogens can be very dangerous organisms, and they do not care about our idealism, sophistry, or ignorance.

The most common reasons anaerobic pathogens might end up in compost tea can be traced directly to improperly made compost. We have listed some basic guidelines for the creation of true thermal compost below:

•The compost pile or bin needs to be turned regularly to encourage the growth of beneficial aerobic microbes, thus discouraging the growth of disease-causing anaerobic organisms.

•The entire pile or batch needs to have been maintained at a temperature exceeding 131°F. (55°C) for over 14 days.

•Tools or machinery used to handle the finished compost

need to be clean, so as to limit re-contamination of the pile, or batch. If you have used a pitch fork or shovel in a manure pile, clean it well before putting it into your finished compost. Please be aware that bacterial biofilm adheres to steel with its own self-manufactured glue.

Certain USDA programs view the making of compost tea as potentially dangerous, even though the USDA has invested very little time or funding for investigation. The studies that do exist tend to be armchair studies skewed towards conventional commercial agricultural dogma.

Performing an Internet search on compost tea will reveal some alarmist literature by various sources, warning of the possible dangers of culturing human pathogens in compost tea. As stated above, the dangers are unquestionably real, but controllable following proper procedures and with adequate knowledge.

However, if we follow the money we can determine where the funding may originate from for many university or private studies—typically large commercial interests. Whether these are the gray-men, men-in-black, blue, pink, or whatever the color *du jour* is, we know one thing; They are frightened of change because they perceive it may result in a loss of their power.

The reader may be justified if it seems we have been over-zealous in our harping about the dangers of the possibility of culturing pathogens in compost tea. It is our intent to inform not to frighten the compost tea maker-to-be. In reality the instances are rare, and **aerobic compost teas are normally quite healthy and safe**. Nature does tend to take care of it's own, and in a healthy ecosystem pathogens are typically consumed by dominant beneficial microbes.

VERMICOMPOST

"Earthworms Are Sacred" Cleopatra

The Greek philosopher Aristotle called earthworms, "The intestines of the soil". Millennium later Charles Darwin was fascinated by earthworms, and spent 39 years studying them. He wrote a book titled, *"The Formation of Vegetable Mould Through the Action of Worms With Observations on Their Habits."*

Evidence suggests that earthworms arose in the Jurassic period, and have been on Earth for at least 120 million years. Scientists believe that most earthworm species in North America were killed during the last ice age by glaciers that creeped down from the Arctic ten to fifty million years ago.

In our modern age earthworms were either purposefully or inadvertently re-introduced to North and South America by early settlers in the 17th and 18th centuries.

Earthworms are members of the phylum Annelida and the class Oligochaeta, of which there are over six thousand known species. Earthworms are classified in the family Lumbricidae, which includes the genera of *Lumbricus, Eisenia, Dendrobaena, and Allobophora*. Even though hundreds of species are associated with these genera, we only use a few as composting worms.

Enlisting worms to make vermicompost that is specifically dedicated to the creation of compost teas is a great idea for gardeners. Earthworms do a very detailed job of it, resulting in a fine, high-nutrient grade of compost.

The creation of vermicompost is biologically a much simpler process than what occurs in a traditional thermal compost pile, which uses a more complex set of organisms to break down organic matter. Given the same basic materials to work with, the two different styles will produce composts yielding their own unique characteristics. Sophisticated gardeners may choose to alternate or blend both styles in their compost tea brews, with the obvious benefit of providing the plants with a more diverse set of microbes and nutrients.

It is important to remember that vermicompost tends to produce **bacterially** dominated compost teas, but is not particularly good for making **fungal** dominated teas. Both types are employed for different purposes, which shall be discussed later.

Earthworms are some of the hardest working creatures on earth, helping to mix and aerate the soil, improving soil structure and water infiltration, modulate pH factors, increasing beneficial microbial activity, and making nutrients more available to plants by breaking down plant and animal material into castings (excrement).

•Worms are capable of creating finished compost out of various materials very quickly—in as little as 60 days.

•Earthworm castings have a neutral pH value (7 pH), regardless of the pH of the soil they are living in. They therefore either help neutralize acidic soils, or acidulate highly alkaline soils.

•Castings have high levels of nitrogen, potassium, phosphorus, magnesium, and trace minerals—all in very plant-available forms

•Castings become food for other organisms, which release potassium, phosphorus, calcium, magnesium, iron, and plant available sulfur into the soil.

•Since worm castings are about 65% organic matter, they help increase the humus content of the soil, which aids in water retention and helps combat compaction.

•Mucus membranes produced by worms encase casting nutrients, causing them to be slowly released as food for plants.

•The optimum carbon to nitrogen (C:N) ratio for plant food is 20:1. Tree leaves tend to have less than optimum C:N levels, such as 42:1 for oaks, and 90:1 for some pine trees. Worms, with a little help from their friends (other organisms) help break down the carbon in leaf litter, finally rendering it close to 20:1, a perfect C:N ratio for the plant's assimilation of nitrogen.

Composting worms digest **most** human pathogens, making vermicompost an excellent choice for the brewing of compost tea. Pathogens, such as Salmonella and E.coli (to name a few) are digested in the intestinal tract of composting worms. The exception concerns cat feces, which may harbor protozoa that are responsible for a human disease called *toxoplasmosis.* Unfortunately, the protozoa can pass through the earthworms' gut unharmed. Therefore, one should not allow any pet feces to enter a worm bin or worm producing compost pile. Earthworms break down the soil into smaller particles, mixing the soil as they work.

The habits of various earthworms can be put into 3 groups:

- The litter dwellers (up to 6 inches deep)
- The shallow soil dwellers (up to 12 inches deep)
- The deep burrowers (up to 6 feet deep)

Our Worm Team Line-up

Nightcrawlers *Lumbricus terrestris*
Nightcrawlers are large worms that have deep burrowing habits, making vertical tunnels as far as six feet into the ground. They feed at night, and get their food (such as leaf litter and mulch), from the surface, dragging it deep into their burrows to feed. Nightcrawlers can live as long as ten years, and are found in Europe, North America, and New Zealand. They are not particularly good for enclosed vermicomposting systems because they feed from the surface, do not like their burrows disturbed, and tend to roam at night-escaping the bin. They are however, frequently found, and welcomed in our outdoor compost piles and garden soils.

Red Wigglers *Eisenia fetida*

Red Wigglers are the darling of the composting world, making them by far the most common worm used in controlled composting systems. They are shallow dwellers, have an upward migration habit, and prefer very rich compost, manure, and decaying plant material for food. Red Wigglers can process large amounts of organic matter very rapidly, and in perfect conditions can eat 1/2 of their body weight in food each day. They are not fussy about their living conditions, tolerating fluctuations in temperature, acidity, and moisture levels better than many other worm species. Contrary to what others have claimed, Red Wigglers can live in outdoor compost piles in temperate climates as long as they have enough oxygen, reasonable moisture levels, and providing they have the space to migrate downwards far enough to avoid high temperatures and freezing conditions. Some growers like to maintain an outdoor population of Red Wigglers as a back-up in the event problems occur in their contained worm bins. However, since they need a lot of organic matter to feed on, Red Wigglers may not survive long in ordinary garden soil. Their cocoons will normally hatch in 5-10 weeks, giving them the ability to be able to double their population in as little as 60 days. Red Wigglers prefer temperatures in the 75-85°range (23-29°C).

Red Tiger Worm *Eisenia andrei*

The Red tiger Worm is a close relative of the Red Wiggler, and has very similar habits, but is not as available commercially.

Redworms *Lumbricus rubellus*

One of the common names used for Redworms is "Red Wigglers", causing Redworms to be oftentimes confused with actual Red Wigglers (*Eisenia fetida*).

Redworms grow up to three inches, live in the top 6-12 inches of the soil, and make good composting worms, except for the fact that their cocoons take 12-16 weeks to hatch (compared to the Red Wigglers 5-10 weeks). Redworms prefer temperatures from 64-72°F. (18-23°C), and make great bait worms because they exude amino acids that fish crave.

Blue Worms *Perionyx excavitus and Perionyx spenceriella*

Various species of Blue Worms are the choice for composting systems in warmer climates, as they do not tolerate cold temperatures well. They are however, voracious feeders rendering them excellent for composting systems. Blue worms have an unusually good ability to feed on animal material as well as decaying plant material. Blue Worms are shallow dwellers and have good regenerative capabilities. While some do have a tendency to roam outside the bins at times, generally Blues are well behaved. One of the more common names is, "Indian Blue" worm. Some are native to Australia.

African Nightcrawler *Eudrilus engeniae*

These giant nightcrawlers are shallow soil dwellers, living mostly in the top 12 inches of the soil. They prefer a warmer temperature range to live in—above 50°F. (10°C.), can be somewhat fussy, and are used by some for composting but are more commonly raised for bait worms.

Worm Bin Basics

One pound of *Eisenia fetida* (Red Wiggler) worms may contain 1000 individuals who, on a good day may eat up to half of their body weight in food. An average human family produces about 1 pound of food scraps per day. Therefore, in ideal conditions two pounds of Red Wiggler worms can deal with the food scraps from one family. However, conditions are not always ideal. In reality, taken on a yearly average, it may take 4-5 pounds of worms to keep up with a family's output, particularly if the family eats plenty of vegetables.

It behooves us to maintain the best environment we can for our worms, which can be difficult at times because they tend to be easy to neglect. We have our priorities. The worms are, frankly, on the bottom of the family food chain. Our worms cannot speak or complain, they can only suffer in quiet dignity if neglected. Like any other animals we choose to take on as our charge, we are honor-bound to protect them.

We have found the worms to be surprisingly tough, but they are sensitive to extremes in temperature and moisture, and susceptible to predation. Some worms occasionally escape from the bins, but most of them are usually trapped inside, or choose to stay there. Unlike in a natural environment, worms in an enclosed bin cannot flee very far from uncomfortable extremes in temperature, moisture, or strong foods such as garlic, onions, or spices. In an ordinary compost pile worms will simply move away from what they do not like. Simply put, worms need to be fussed over when raised in enclosed bins.

Predators

Because worms are themselves an excellent food coveted by birds, moles, voles, mice and snakes, we protect them by raising them in bins designed to keep predators out. There are recipes in some of the worm books for preparing worms for human consumption. We shall consider that option only as a last resort.

Temperature

We recommend using long stemmed thermometers for maintaining comfortable temperatures for your worms. Red Wiggler worms are tolerant of temperatures in the 40-120° F. range (5-50°C), but are most active at about 85° F. (32°C)

Once, in sub-freezing temperatures we observed them balling-up to conserve body heat. All of the worms in a small plastic 4-tray bin had congregated into a softball sized sphere, like a ball of herring in the ocean. In spite of the admirable survival technique they eventually would have frozen if we had not moved them to a warmer location. Large stationary worm bins can be mulched or surrounded by straw or other insulating materials to protect the worms from the cold, or tray-type worm systems can be moved into a building where it is warmer.

Mobility is an advantage inherent to stackable tray worm bins. Inside a building, one 40 watt light bulb under a covered worm bin will provide a surprising amount of heat.

We must also protect the worms from excessive heat. In the warmer months the bins should be placed in a shady location with plenty of ventilation around the bin. Once again, we have observed the worms surprising durability. The same worms that formed a "ball of herring" in the winter survived 106° F. (41°C) ambient temperatures the following summer. Realistically there was probably some die-back during both of those extremes in temperatures.

Vibration

Worms have a low tolerance for persistent vibrations emanating from refrigerators, air conditioners, heat pumps, furnaces, railroads, and other mechanical sources.

Like any other organism, they are also agitated while in the presence of magnetic fields associated with large electric motors, power lines, audio speakers, audio amplifiers, and powerful lunar cycles.

Moisture

Worms prefer a damp but not wet environment. Moisture is extracted from the food scraps placed in the bin, some of which will condense on the inside of the roof, or fall into the liquid collection tray. A diligent wormer will monitor his or her bins regularly to make certain they do not dry out, and are protected from rain and excessive moisture.

Acidity

One of the truly remarkable characteristics of worms is that no matter what they eat, their castings end up at about 7pH. As mentioned earlier, worms are an acidity modulator. Their castings will either help make highly alkaline soils more acidic, or acidic soils more alkaline. As most gardeners know, soil pH has a direct affect on the way nitrogen is assimilated by plants. Less nitrogen is available to plants growing in acidic soils.

Worms do not prefer to eat highly acidic foods, such as citrus peels and coffee grounds. One can add a little garden lime to counter the effect of acidic foods, but that also may be a shock to the worms if too much is added. It is best to bleed it in slowly, by adding lime to your compost bucket prior to putting that in the worm bin.

We save our eggshells. When we have collected about 1/2 gallon of them they are pulverized in the kitchen blender with some water. Worms cannot deal with them if they are too coarse. The slurry can be dumped directly into the worm bin or compost bucket, adding a natural source of calcium.

Worm Bedding

Bedding is placed into the bottom of a bin or tray as a kind of neutral medium for the worms to relax in. Bedding material needs to be damp, so that if you squeeze a handful of it a drop or two of water will come out of it. Bedding comes in many forms, but will need to fit the following criteria:

- ●Retains moisture
- ●Ventilate well
- ●Good moisture drainage
- ●Not a high-protein food source
- ●Aged past the stage where it will heat-up (grass clippings)
- ●A good carbon source for bacteria

Coconut Coir

Alas, the Cadillac of bedding materials is also the most expensive. Coconut coir comes off of the husk of the coconut, and is a renewable resource. It must however, be imported from tropical areas, thus the cost, which is not prohibitive, but we are comparing it with other bedding materials—some of which are free. Coconut coir is clean, odor-free, ventilates well, retains moisture, and is usually about 6.2 pH. To get your worms off to a good start, the budding worm grower should consider buying some coconut coir.

Peat Moss

Peat moss bedding has been used extensively by worm growers, has many characteristics similar to coconut coir, but is a bit on the acidic side. Peat moss is good to use in a blend with less acidic bedding materials. One can also soak it with a little lime or eggshell slurry prior to adding it to the bin. It would be wise to soak the peat moss for several days to allow the calcium to integrate in well. Liquid calcium is also an option to consider when using peat moss as a bedding material. Liquid calcium is used in agricultural drip irrigation systems.

Canadian peat moss is preferred over American peat moss because of impurities associated with some American peat moss products.

Newspaper and Telephone books

Regular newsprint (not glossy color paper) works well for worm bedding as long as it is mixed with other bedding materials to keep it from compacting. The black ink is not a problem. It can be torn or cut into strips before wetting and added to the bin. With tray-type systems, newspaper on the bottom of the trays will help to insulate them in the colder months of the year.

Wood chips & sawdust

Fine wood chips or sawdust make good bedding especially if blended with other bedding material. Larger chips may remain in a finished tray of worm castings, which is not a plus for using those castings for making compost tea. Sawdust may be a wiser choice of bedding material for the compost tea maker than wood chips.

Avoid using too much sawdust from conifers, that have acidic pitch in the wood (firs and pines). Also, do not use sawdust from cedars, or other aromatic species. Those trees have aromatic oils in them specifically to protect themselves from insects. The oils are an irritant to worms. Use sawdust from deciduous species like alder, oak, maple, beech, or non-fragrant conifers like hemlock or spruce.

Leaves

If leaves are completely broken down (almost compost) , they can be used mixed with other bedding materials. Some leaves, like walnut leaves, have strong tannins that may be an irritant to worms.

Stationary Worm Bin Design

What is a worm bin? A worm bin can be many things. Worm growers, by nature being rather down-to-earth characters, have exhibited ingenious and admirable non-denominational open-mindedness when choosing the vessels destined to be christened as "worm bins".

Plastic storage totes, old camping coolers, wooden boxes, discarded cabinet drawers, and burnt-out refrigerators may all provide refuge for our squirmy friends. The list goes on, possibly into eternity—the perpetual medicine-wheel of worm bins.

Composting worms are shallow dwellers, not requiring more than 3 inches to live and feed in. Even though worms don't really need the extra depth in a large stationary-type bin, the extra depth does provide places for the worms to retreat to during extreme temperature fluctuations.

Whatever container the worm grower chooses needs to be well ventilated. This can be done by drilling 1/2" holes every 5 inches on a rough grid on the side and the bottom of the container. We prefer 1/2" holes, because they are too small for rodents to squeeze through.

A scrap of plywood will serve as a functional lid, which should keep out rainwater but ventilate to a certain degree as well.

A single large deep bin may not be the best choice for the compost tea maker. At what point in a large bin does the worm grower decide the bin is filled with pure worm castings? Growers using large bins will need to have more than one container if they want to continue to add food scraps, and at the same time allow the food in another bin to be completely consumed by the worms. The rotational system has worked for many growers, particularly on a large scale.

Tray-Type Worm Bin Systems

Tray-type systems are becoming increasingly popular because of their efficiency and mobility. The idea behind a tray-type system is to utilize from 3-5 shallow, stackable trays with screen bottoms to form a composite bin. When the trays are stacked together, the worms can move freely though the screens into any tray they choose to be in. Eventually the bottom tray becomes filled with pure worm castings, while food scraps are still being added to a tray above.

The trays can be rotated at the discretion of the worm grower. When the worms have filled the bottom tray with castings, the grower harvests the contents from it, then uses it as a fresh tray with new bedding and worm food. It is a very flexible rotational system, and mobile. If the bin is too heavy to move, one can grab one tray at a time and re-assemble it elsewhere.

We like tray-type systems for making compost tea because when the bottom tray is full of castings, it is controlled and undeniable pure. All one has to do is pick out the stray worms before using the castings to make compost tea.

Worm Bin Liquid

One needs to orient the container to allow the capture of the liquid that drips out of the bottom of any worm bin. The liquid has value as a fertilizer as long as it has not turned anaerobic and smells stinky. There are some who refer to the liquid as "compost tea", but we refrain from calling it that because it is somewhat of an uncontrolled substance. It may, in many cases serve as a superb fertilizer, but the experts strongly recommend discarding it if it has become anaerobic. If so, it should be poured out somewhere that will not bacterially impact your plants.

In light of that bit of wisdom, it's a good idea to maintain your liquid collection tray diligently. Most tray-type worm bin systems have a spigot on the liquid collection tray. Many vermiculturests leave the spigot open with a cup under it to catch the liquid as it drips out. That way, it's easy to remember to grab the cup, smell it, and use it accordingly.

Ordering worms

Suppliers of worms may grow and sell different species of worms, since many home growers or small businesses grow worms for fish bait. As you may have noticed, there is some confusion between the common names and the scientific names for worm species. When ordering worms, use the scientific species name to avoid any confusion. You will need 1 or 2 pounds of worms for a 15 ½" commercial tray-type plastic bin, or 2 to 3 pounds for our larger 24" design. If you are on a tight budget, you could start with only one pound, but it will simply take several months longer to fully populate your bin.

Be prepared to wait for a few weeks to receive your worms. Suppliers harvest on a monthly schedule and ship the worms based on their schedule. Some suppliers are actually brokers that do not grow worms, but deal with many growers. Those companies are good to order from because they will arrange to have worms drop-shipped to a customer from the grower who is closest to the customer. Shipping worms is sensitive business, and it is prudent if the overall shipping time is minimized. Some growers will simply not ship during seasonal temperature extremes. The buyer of the worms should use caution and common sense as well. For example; if you live in Minnesota, do not order worms in January, or do not have worms sent to Phoenix in August. In the USA, worms are always shipped via USPS, who is the only carrier willing to handle live animals in small packages. For the most part, the US postal service is efficient, and handles packages relatively carefully, so the worms usually arrive in good condition. Examine your worms to make sure they are alive when they arrive.

Caring For Your Worms

Before your worms arrive, be prepared to put them to bed in their new home as soon as they do. Your new worm family will be under considerable stress, so at that point in time make it a priority to take care of them. Your worm bin should already be assembled and prepared.

•Pre-soak your bedding materials if necessary. Coconut coir should be soaked for at least 4 hours in chlorine-free water. If you have only municipal water-boil it to get the chlorine out.

•With a tray system you will begin by using only one tray that is destined to become the bottom tray for awhile.

•Start by putting a piece of newspaper on the bottom of the tray. The paper will keep the worms from falling through the screen into the liquid below.

•Add your pre-soaked bedding materials to total about 1/3 of the depth of the tray. A mixture of bedding materials is good, because it provides a more complex set of nutrients for your worms.

•Add two coffee cups full of ordinary garden soil to the tray. The soil provides grit, minerals, and microbes to the blend. Do not use compost for this, as you may be introducing unwanted guests into the bin such as: slug or snail babies, mites etc.

•Put the worms and the bedding material they arrived with on top of your newly prepared bedding in the tray.

•Put the roof on the tray. Allow the worms time to work their way into the bedding.

•The next morning feed your worms breakfast. Avoid putting any experimental food into the bin at first (like your mornings French roast coffee grounds). Show the worms how hospitable you can be by fussing over them a bit. Put your best foot forward. Chop or blend up some vegetable scraps, lettuce, melons, green tea, kelp or seaweed (no salt), and distribute that into the tray. Better yet, make yourself some carrot juice and give them the pulp. Carrot pulp is worm *caviar*. Make it easy for your worms the first week and feed them some comfort food. After that, feed your worms twice per week until you observe they can handle more food.

Add your second tray

•Add the next tray. When about 70% of the scraps in the first tray has been processed by the worms, and it is full of material, you may put the next tray on top of it. Make certain that the screen from the second tray is in contact with the material from the first tray. That way the worms can crawl up into the second tray when they are ready to do so . To re-iterate, we call that their "upward migration habit."

•Do not put any paper in the bottom of the second tray. The worms must be able to move freely through the screen. They will move up to feed, and back down to breed!

•Throw a little bedding material, some garden soil, and some food into the second tray. Put the lid on the assembly. You now have two trays working for you.

•Continue feeding the worms in the second tray until you can add the third tray

Add your third tray

•Once they have finished with about 50% of the third tray you should be able to harvest the contents of the bottom tray. The worms will continue to go back down into the bottom tray until there is no more food left there. It will be solid worm castings! Worm castings are coffee-colored, fine-textured, but soft with humus, and have little perceptible odor.

•Pick the stray worms out of the castings. When the worms are completely finished with the first, bottom tray there may be a few lazy worms in it, but no cocoons. By that time they will be laying their young in the second tray.

Rotation

•The contents of the second tray will now become in the bottom tray position.

Commercially available tray-type worm bins

Practical 15 ½ inch plastic tray systems are available on the retail market in 3,4, and 5 tray models. They typically come with a ventilated lid, stand, a dedicated liquid collection tray with a spigot, landscaping cloth, and enough coconut coir bedding to get started. One of these lightweight designed worm bins will not really process enough food scraps for an entire family, but are becoming popular in urban environments and for those who want compact, attractive units capable of producing high-quality worm castings. There are growers that are creating first-class soil for their plants on the balconies of their flats on the 30th floor!

Worm Tray Design

We have designed large worm trays that are easy to build, cost half as much as a plastic tray system, and will hold over 1.4 cubic feet of castings per tray. If you use 3 trays as we are recommending, the bin will hold 4.2 cubic feet of material. Each tray measures 24" x 24" x 5.5", and is designed to be built with very commonly available materials in the USA.

The concept is so simple that readers in other countries should be able to ad-lib, using material sizes common to their own locality.

These larger volume worm trays are easy to build yet small enough to handle. The frames are constructed with common 2x6 lumber with 1/4" mesh galvanized screen bottoms. Obviously, these trays could also be used for sifting soil.

We have included materials lists and cut lists for both 3 trays and one tray. We recommend building 3 trays that will stack on one another. If using concrete blocks as a pedestal, the entire 3 tray assembly will stand 25" tall, and be 2 feet wide and 2 feet deep. Your 3-stack worm bin assembly can have a plastic tray, bucket, or stainless steel cooking pot underneath to catch the extra liquid.

Worm Bin Lid

The lid can be as simple as a piece of scrap plywood or Styrofoam insulation board. It needs to be opaque, protect the bin from rain, and ideally provide some ventilation as well. If it is over-sized by several inches the entire bin can be shielded from both the rain and the sun. A single piece of plywood could be cut to 28" x 28", which would leave an 2" overhang overall.

The lumber lengths could be cut at the lumber store where it is purchased-for a nominal fee-if you do not have a saw capable of making square cuts.

Tools needed

- Power drill-cordless or corded
- Screwdriver tip to match the screws you choose
- 3/16" or 4mm drill bit
- Wire cutters for the 1/4" screen
- Hammer
- Optional saw to cut boards to length

Material list for 3 trays

- 3—8 ft. 2x6 standard framing lumber (untreated)
- 1—8 ft. 1x2 utility lumber (usually pine)
- 6 ft. x 24" 1/4"x 1/4" galvanized hardware cloth screen. Enough for 3—24"x 24" pieces
- 1 lb. 3" galvanized dry-wall type screws
- 20—1 1/2" galvanized dry-wall type screws
- 1 lb. 1" roofing nails or small horseshoe nails
- 4—Concrete blocks

Cut list for 3 trays

- 6—2x6 cut to 24"
- 6—2x6 cut to 21"
- 6—1x2 cut to 15 7/8"
- 3—galvanized hardware cloth pieces cut to 24"x24"

Materials list for 1 tray

- 1—8ft. 2X6 standard framing lumber (untreated)
- 2—15 7/8" 1x2 utility
- 1—24"x24" 1/4"x1/4" galvanized hardware cloth screen
- 12—3" galvanized dry-wall screws
- 6—1 ½" galvanized dry-wall screws

Cut list for 1 tray

- 2—2x6 cut to 24"
- 2—2x6 cut to 21"
- 2—1X2 cut to 15 7/8
- 1—24"x24" galvanized hardware cloth screen

Construction tips from a pro woodworker
Insist on purchasing only straight 2x6 boards

- Once again, if you do not have access to a saw that will make clean, square cuts (power miter saw, radial arm saw, or table saw) have the pieces cut at the lumber store when you buy the 2x6. Square cuts will help your trays stack flat.

- Pre-drill all holes for screws with a 3/16 drill bit. However, you should only drill through the boards that you wish to attach to another board. Example: Drill 3—3/16" holes through the 15 7/8" handles, but not into the 2x6 you are attaching them to. Pre- drilling may seem like an unnecessary step to some, but it will result in a more accurate, cleaner looking job with no splitting. If the lumber splits, the trays will not stack flat.

- You will pre-drill through both ends of the 24" 2x6. Locate the outside holes 1" from each edge of the board, and ¾" in from the end.

- Screw the frames together on a flat surface (floor), and make sure the top and bottom edges are flush. If after driving in the first screw you are unsatisfied with the boards not being lined up, put a block under the lower board and hit the higher board with a hammer—hard. If there is only one screw in it, it will move a little. Then remove the block and drive in the other two screws.

- The 15 7/8" handles are important. Later, when you are working with the trays you will be glad you installed them.

•Locate the handles flush with the top edge of the 24" 2x6. By the way, 15 7/8' is not a magic number, just a practical number. One 8 foot 1x2 cut into 6 pieces will actually yield six 15 7/8" pieces (not 16"), because we have to figure for the thickness of the saw blade. The actual length of the handles is not critical.

•Fasten the galvanized screen onto the bottom of each tray with the 1 inch wide-headed roofing nails or horseshoe nails. The nails can be about 2" apart, but not too close to an edge or an end so as not to split the wood. Use the screen itself to make sure each 2x6 frame is square. Start by fastening the factory edge of the screen to one board, lining it up perfectly with that board. The screen is absolutely square, so look at how it lines up with the rest of the 2x6 frame. Set (but not drive in) a nail on the opposite board you just nailed into, adjust the frame to match the screen, then drive in the nail. Granted, this is not rocket science, but these little tips will help you to construct trays that are flat and square, making them stack well. The screen may tend to sag a bit, but that is OK. The liquid will then drip out of the middle of the tray.

•These 24" x 24" trays are heavy when wet and filled with compost. Smaller trays can be made by reducing the 21" boards to 17". The resulting finished tray size would then be 24" x 20". The galvanized 1/4" screen sometimes comes in a 5 ft. roll (60"), which is enough screen for three 24" x 20" trays.

3—24" x 24" Worm Trays
The One Quart Mason Jar Is For Size Perspective

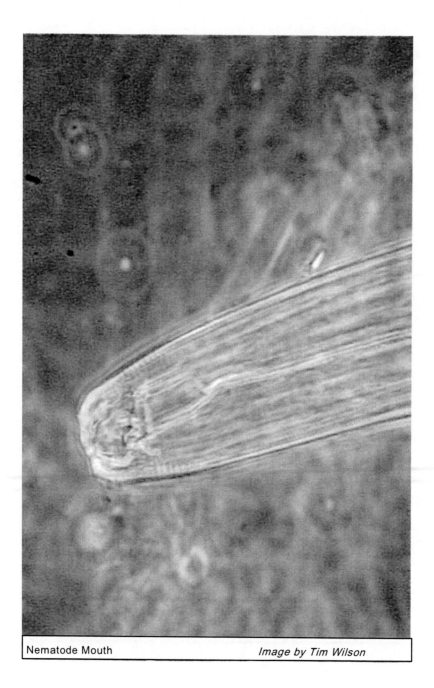

Nematode Mouth   *Image by Tim Wilson*

Interview with Kelan Moynagh of Yelm Earthworm & Castings Farm

What got you started in the earthworm business?

When we bought this business, we wanted to do something that was both good for the planet and a profitable business too. That was in 2005, really at the beginning of the green movements' surge.

So it was already a functioning business?

Well, the previous owners had their ups and downs, but really their focus was different than ours. There have actually been several similar businesses on this site before ours. Originally, it was an organic mushroom farm, then a soil operation, and finally became devoted to Vermiculture.

You are 100% organic aren't you?

Yes, we are a WSCA certified organic food program registered worm grower. We have worked very hard to maintain one of the best standards in the industry.

What are your main products?

We sell worms, various blends of earthworm castings, compost, and soil for different uses. Our trademarked product is called Barefoot Soil, which is a blend of 60% earthworm castings and 40% humus compost. We also carry products associated with earthworms and soils.

Do you make the humus compost? You mean thermal compost—right?

Correct, and yes we do make the thermal compost on site. We have a

*dedicated rotating sifter just for the compost. It passes through 1/4"
screen, so it comes out pretty fine.*

What is the thermal compost made out of?
Horse manure.

That's it? What do you use for a carbon source?
*Well, the horse manure we get has pellets in it. A lot of stables use the
compressed sawdust pellets instead of wood chips now because they
absorb moisture better, and it's great for us because they break down
into fine compost.*

How do you turn it?
*With the front loader. We usually have about 100 yards going at any
time*

What is your vermicompost capacity?
We have eight bays with 70 to 100 yards in each one.

What species of worm do you use?
Red wigglers-Eisenia fetida

What do you use for bedding?
*We use dairy cow manure for both the bedding and the food. You can see
that 8 foot worm bin on the end of the row. We all bring any scraps we
get to put in it but it doesn't amount to much. Most of the composting
takes place in piles on the concrete. We just keep adding more manure
to the top until we cannot get the loader in here any more.*

Doesn't some dairy cow manure have non-organic products in
it?
*You bet, but our source is hormone free and antibiotic free. Some worm
growers have had some serious problems with manure from dairies. We
had to help a big grower in California repopulate their piles with three*

hundred pounds of worms from ours. They were not sure what caused the death of their worms, but we heard that some big feed-lot dairies will still use formaldehyde on the hooves of the cows even though they are not supposed to. Worms are resilient, but not that tough.

That thermometer is reading 120° F (49°C) Isn't that kind of hot?
Its a 2 ft. long thermometer, and pretty deep into the pile. The worms will go where they like in the pile. Right now they are closer to the top. I think the ideal temperature for them is about 85-90°F. (29-32°) They can handle it up to about 130° F. (55°C).

How about the low range?
They can survive freezing temperatures but it slows them down a lot. In fact, I think that below 45°F. they do not breed, lay cocoons, and the cocoons already there will not hatch. That's something you will not read in a worm book. It is based on our experience last winter, when because of unusually cold weather, our piles dropped down to 45°F. for much of the winter. In the spring when we harvested we were getting only 200 worms per pound, but big fat ones. Usually we get about 700 to 1000 smaller worms per pound. I think we harvested the adults that had lived through the winter, had gotten larger, but not bred.

That makes sense. There are some pot worms in here (little white worms). What do you think about those?
Pot worms are beneficials. I think they help begin the process of breaking down the material.

I have noticed them in the beginning feeding on kitchen scraps. I have wondered if they prefer a more acidic environment. Perhaps when the pH goes up as the compost matures they disappear.
It's possible. You are asking better questions than most I give the tour to.

Well I am supposed to be an expert, but honestly just writing a book does not make one so. I feel like I am barely scratching the surface. There is so much to learn.

Yeah, we learn more every year.

How long does it take to process one of these piles?

It depends, but usually about 16 months. I know they say it can happen in 60 days but that would be under IDEAL conditions. If these worms always ate ½ their body weight in food every day we would really be in business.

So, if you don't mind me asking, how is the business?

It's OK, but it could be better. It's surprising how long it is taking people to realize how potent worm castings are, particularly in this state (Washington). In California it is a thriving business. The concept has to first change from something you put on your plants to give them fertilizer, to something you add to provide more microbial life. The universities taught that NPK way of thinking for too long.

NPK?

You know, nitrogen, potassium, phosphorus and clay. That's all soil was. Minerals. Dead. You know some of the nurseries won't handle our products because our soils blatantly have bacteria in them? The nurseries want all of their soil sterile. What they do not realize is that these are good, beneficial microbes that help stave off the undesirable ones. And pathogens. Did you know that worms give off a secretion that kills human pathogens? They do not even have to pass through the gut. That's another one not in most books.

Really!, I didn't know that.

There is even more resistance to compost tea. We make it here in that big fermenter and sell it on the weekends, but it's slow to catch on. I tried to tell the dairies that they can spray it on the walls of the milking area to get rid of the flies but they won't listen. There is quite a bit of negative scuttle about it in the market place, and the master gardeners are banned from talking about it. They are funded by WSU.

I know, that's a good one. Where are we—in the old Soviet Union? I am refusing to address that in my book. I don't want to get involved in the drama. I've been staying focused on the science, which is so clear. You'd think we were living amongst Neanderthals or something.

Aren't we? LOL

Are fresh castings more microbially potent that old ones?

Definitely.

OK, Lets say I harvest fresh castings in December, but I don't want to use them until spring. What is the best way to store castings for a few months and keep the microbes happy?

Above all they need to stay moist, but with some ventilation. So ideally the castings may require some maintenance to stay vital. You would be surprised what passes for worm castings in the retail market. Some products are actually heated and dried. There can't be much life left in it.

Do you have any other worm growing tips for amateurs?

The finer chopped their food is the better, and once again, keep them moist. They actually like it a lot wetter than the books say. We have observed many times that they migrate to where the water is. Those little stackable worm bins can get too dry easily. Pour some water on them, they love it, but keep that drain valve open on the bottom tray.

On that subject, what do you think about the leachate that drips out of the bins?

There have been some good results from the use of it, but still it's really a wild card. As long as it has not turned anaerobic its OK, but one never really knows unless you send a sample to the lab. And since compost tea is unstable, the lab report would be outdated by the time you got it.

Thanks for sharing all of the info Kelan

It was my pleasure

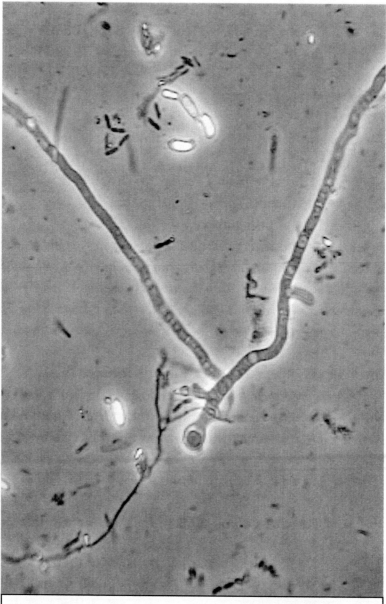

Fungal Hyphae   *Image by Tim Wilson*

TRADITIONAL THERMAL COMPOST

In a traditional compost pile, materials can be broken down into soil quite rapidly. As far as we know, the bacteria responsible for most of the consuming do not have corporate meetings, engage in lengthy studies, or charge exorbitant consulting fees for their expertise. They do however, work together in a kind of relay race, passing the baton from one type of bacteria to another, finally leaving the completion of the composting to fungi, worms, and bugs. Worms typically make their entrance into the game once the pile cools down below 100°F. (38°C), after the thermophilic microorganisms have finished.

Endeavoring to apply human morality to this microbial race may not be wise, as at different stages in the game players will often times eat other contestants, or the dead remains of them.

The team is made up of four different types of bacteria, listed in the temperature ranges they are most active in, and in their order of participation in the race:

- Psychorophilic bacteria—below 70°F. (21°C)
- Mesophilic bacteria—70 to 113°F. (21-41°C)
- Thermophilic bacteria—115 to 170°F. (43-77°C)
- Actinomycetes bacteria—below 75°F. (24°C)

Making Thermal Compost

What is actually needed to make thermal compost?
- Organic materials
- Moisture
- Oxygen
- Heat

Organic materials

Organic materials can be divided into two categories: "brown" and "green". Aged, brown materials are high in carbon, while fresh green materials are high in nitrogen. Achieving the proper balance between the two categories is the key to successful composting. This is referred to as the carbon to nitrogen ratio (C:N). The ideal C:N ratio for a beginning compost pile is in the 25:1—30:1 range.

Brown materials high in carbon include: leaves (40:1—80:1), sawdust (500:1), paper (170:1), wood chips, twigs, and branches.

Green materials high in nitrogen include: grass clippings (19:1), fresh weeds, kitchen scraps, and alfalfa meal.

If one wants to make a bacterially dominated compost, green materials are favored. If fungal-dominated compost is needed, more brown materials are used.

Moisture

The correct amount of moisture one should endeavor to maintain in a compost pile could be described as slightly damp. Microorganisms need an adequate amount of moisture or they will go into dormancy or die. Too much moisture may create problems as well. It should not be dripping wet on the bottom of the pile.

Oxygen

We want to encourage the growth of aerobic, oxygen-loving microbes that break down carboniferous and nitrogenous materials. Compost piles can become anaerobic, and decay will occur under those conditions as well, but for the purpose of making compost tea we want aerobic compost, which breaks down much quicker anyway. As has already been stated, anaerobic compost may harbor pathogens, but also produce alcohols and other compounds which are harmful to plants.

Turning the compost pile or rotating your compost tumbler regularly is important because you are both mixing and adding air at the same time. It should be noted that turning can either increase or decrease the temperature of the compost pile depending on what stage it is in.

Heat

Heat is generated by the metabolic activity in the pile itself, mostly from bacteria. As the heat increases, changes in the guard naturally occur when the baton is passed from the mesophilic to the thermophilic type bacteria. The first two stages take place very rapidly, heating up to 135 F. (57C) in as little as 24 hours. At this stage, complex carbohydrates are broken down, and cellulose is broken down into glucose. If the compost has not heated up to 135F. (57C) in 3 days, turn it more and/or add more green material like fresh grass clippings.

The compost should be held at between 140-150°F. (60-66°C) for a few days to ensure the demise of pathogens and weed seeds. Avoid letting the compost temperature rise above 155°F. (68°C), as at that temperature carbon will begin to burn off. At that point, if necessary, the pile may be cooled by turning.

As the compost slowly begins to cool down, protozoa, nematodes, arthropods and worms begin to work in it as well.

The compostee might consider using commercially available compost inoculums, especially if the intent is to use the compost to make compost tea. These products contain nutrients that help boost the process along, and keep our microbial comrades happy.

Compost recipes

As the reader may notice, there is no manure in these recipes, which will certainly work perfectly well in compost destined to be applied directly to the ground. For the purpose of making compost with the intent to create compost tea we have chosen recipes without manure to limit the potential of having pathogens in the finished tea. This is, admittedly, a very conservative approach. The reader may have observed that Yelm Earthworm & Castings Farm is creating thermal compost out of *pure* horse manure + wood pellets, and producing pathogen-free compost tea out of it. The recipes presented here are not the *only* way to create good thermal compost. Once again, many roads lead to compost tea!

Why is one recipe for "bacterial" and another for "fungal" compost?

The compost tea maker has choices: a bacterially dominated tea, a fungal dominated tea, or a bacterial/fungal blend. The best place to start to create one style or another is in the compost pile or worm bin. Whatever aerobic organisms that are already present in the compost will be multiplied during the tea brewing process.

The general consensus amongst tea makers is that it is much easier to create bacterially dominated teas than fungal dominated ones. Bacteria are usually present in large numbers in a well composted pile or in worm castings, but fungal bio-mass may be low. Therefore, it is wise to encourage the growth of fungi in the compost pile to ensure an adequate amount of fungi in the tea.

A general purpose, wide spectrum bacterial/fungal tea may

be a practical choice for a variety of applications.

Rock Phosphate

The addition of rock phosphate to any compost pile is highly recommended, particularly in areas that receive plenty of rainfall. Those areas tend to have soils that are phosphorus deficient. This natural source of phosphorus and minerals will help the microbes as they feed, and in turn, the microbes will integrate the phosphate into the soil. Rock phosphate is widely available.

Pre-activating your fungal tea batch

Some find it difficult to create a strict fungal dominated tea, or even a balanced bacterial/fungal tea because they simply do not have compost with enough fungal bio-mass content. You can multiply the fungi in a small batch of compost a few days prior to using it by giving the fungi some food, and keeping it warm.

Mix 4 spoonfuls of fine oatmeal (oat flour), powdered baby oatmeal, soybean meal, or oat bran with each cup of your slightly moist compost. Put it in a container and keep it at 80°F. (27°C.) for 5 days. Do not stir, mix or disturb the compost. You should see visible fungal mycelia in 3-5 days, at which time you can use it to make a batch of strong fungal dominated tea.

Compost Recipes

Basic bacterial compost recipe
- 50% green grass clipping
- 30% brown material
- 20% alfalfa meal

EZ bacterial/fungal compost recipe
- 3 cubic yards brown material
- 50 pounds alfalfa meal

Basic fungal compost recipe
- 50% brown material
- 40% green material
- 10% alfalfa meal

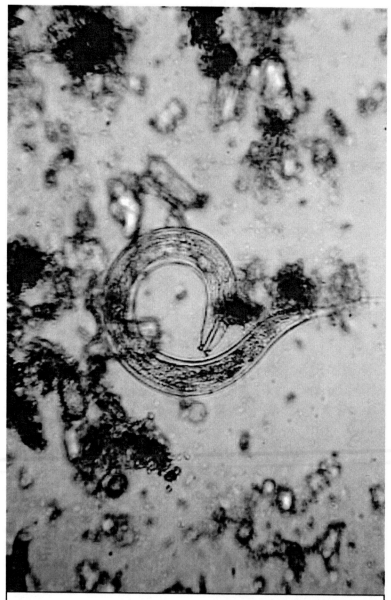

Nematode   *Image by Tim Wilson*

COMPOST TEAS

Compost tea is simply an aerated brewed extract of compost in water. Depending on the intended application, the tea can be tailored to have either more fungus, or more bacteria in it. We have already discussed how the tea-maker can begin the process of creating one style or another by starting in the compost pile or worm bins. The next step is to brew the tea in a way that favors either more fungus or more bacterial growth. When we brew a batch of compost tea, in addition to possibly using compost that favors bacteria or fungi, we can add more or less nutrients of specific kinds that will also help create a fungal dominated or a bacterial dominated tea.

Fungal dominated teas

Fungi help generate more acidity (lower pH) in the soil. Old growth forest soils contain some of the highest levels of fungal bio-mass, which encourages higher acidity and lower nitrogen levels. We can observe what kind of plants thrive in those conditions, namely: trees, shrubs, and perennials. When brewing a compost tea for the roots of those kind of plants, we ideally choose to make a brew that is fungal dominated.

An adequate amount of beneficial fungal bio-mass is needed in teas to help control many fungal diseases on the leaves, branches, and trunks of plants. In fact, fungal dominated tea is the tea of choice when there is pressure from fungal diseases such as powdery mildew and downy mildew.

Bacterial dominated teas

Bacteria produce alkaline compounds lower in acidity. Soils that have been disturbed more often, such as annually roto-tilled soils tend to have higher levels of bacteria than fungus. Bacterial dominated soils are typically higher in pH, lower in acidity, therefore will release more plant available nitrogen. Vegetables, annuals, and grasses favor bacterially dominated soils, so when we make a compost tea for those applications we tailor our brew to be more bacterially dominated.

Balanced fungal/bacterial blend teas

Another option, very commonly used, is a balanced fungal/bacterial tea blend, which works well in most applications. A fungal/bacterial blend is a practical option one can use as a general tonic for perennials, trees, annuals and gardens.

Fungal dominated compost teas are used both in the soil and as foliar applications for:

- Trees
- Perennials
- Shrubs
- Orchards
- Vineyards

Bacterial dominated compost teas are used both in the soil and as foliar applications for:

- Vegetables
- Gardens
- Annuals
- Lawns

Already reasonably healthy horticultural environments will benefit from regular applications of compost teas. However, when disease problems occur, specific diseases can be controlled by either bacterial or fungal dominated teas, or a blend of both. We have much to learn regarding what kinds of teas are best to use in specific situations. We have included a short list of plant diseases that compost tea applications have shown to be successful with.

Some diseases controlled by fungal dominated compost teas

- Powdery mildew *(Phytophthora spp.)*
- Downy mildew *(Sclerophthora spp.)*
- Gray mold *(Botrytis cinerea)*
- Take-all *(Gaeumannomyces spp.)*
- Gray snow mold *(Typhula spp.)*
- Pink snow mold *(Microdochium spp.)*
- Red thread *(Laetisaria spp.)*
- Crown and root rots *(Pythium spp.)*
- Brown patch *(Rhizoctonia solani)*
- Summer patch *(Magnaporthe* spp.)
- Rusts *(Puccinia* spp.)

Some diseases controlled by bacterial dominated compost teas

- Dollar spot *(Sclerotinia spp.)*
- Necrotic ring spot *(Leptosphaeria spp.)*
- Yellow patch *(Rhizoctonia cerealis)*
- Leaf spots *(Curvularia* spp., *Bipolaris* spp.)
- Pink patch *(Limonomyces* spp.)
- Stripe smut *(Ustilago* spp.)

Where is compost tea used?

- Gardens
- Farms
- Lawns
- Golf courses
- Orchards
- Nurseries
- Vineyards

Farms

Today, some of the best work with compost tea is being done in the organic and bio-dynamic commercial sectors. Scientists have studied and tested compost teas, but it is the professional growers who are really finding out what works in their particular situations and environments. This is applied science at it's best, where it is the *need* that drives commercial growers to experiment. Researchers are working closely with the growers, especially studying lab samples, but since the chemistry is so complex, the few researchers cannot really keep up with what the growers are doing, especially since more people are using compost teas every day.

Lawns

The soils resting underneath most American lawns are microbial graveyards. Homeowners are discovering the benefits of compost tea applications which are helping to revitalize their lawns. Golf courses are spearheading the practical research in that sector. Greens keepers are artists, representing the cutting edge of lawn and grass growing technology. Lawns will benefit from applications of balanced fungal/bacterial teas.

Vineyards

A key sector that is playing an important role in the practical development of compost teas is the wine grape industry, who are on an eternal quest for perfection. The international wine industry is huge, and the competition fierce.

Only about 3% of all the vineyards in the world are devoted to the production of table grapes. The remainder—millions of hectares—are devoted to the growing of the *Vitis vinifera* species wine grapes.

The quality of the grapes is paramount in creating a quality wine. Consider this; there are recently made bottles of wine that sell for as much as $8000 each, and $100 bottles are not uncommon. If it takes about ten clusters of grapes to make one $100 bottle of wine, then each *cluster* that goes into that bottle has a potential market value of $10 each. OK, those are expensive grapes. $8000 bottles are rare, but each small *grape* that is used to make that bottle from Burgundy, France is worth about $18. Wow! Obviously, the wine industry has license to go to extremes.

Viticulturists are finding they can increase the over-all health of their vineyards without the undesirable side effect of increased vine vigor. The fact that there is a direct relationship between the quality of the grapes and the quality of the wine made from those grapes should not surprise us. The growers and wine makers know that the healthier the vineyards are the better their wine will be. Vineyards will benefit from both foliar applications of fungal dominated teas in the growing season, and an annual soil drenching with fungal tea in the early dormant season.

A key element in vineyard soils is Boron, which is very important for the development of roots, shoots, leaves and fruit. Soils low in organic matter—sandy soils in particular—are not good reservoirs for Boron. The organic matter along with the soil flora and fauna are mainly responsible for holding Boron in the rhizosphere in humid climates.

Gardens & Flowers

Home gardeners are finding multiple uses for compost teas, both bacterial and fungal. Gardeners have found that compost tea helps encourage plants to tolerate wider temperature ranges, allowing a longer growing season. If you love beautiful flowers, reward them with compost teas! Perennials will benefit from fungal dominated teas, or a balanced fungal/bacterial blend, while annuals will grow larger and produce even more dynamic colors after receiving soil drenches of bacterial dominated teas. Field trials have proven that the root systems of *any* plant tends to be healthier and grows much deeper after repeated applications of compost tea.

Equipment

Compost tea is made by pumping air into water into which compost and nutrients have been added. This can be accomplished in a myriad of ways, either by using a commercially available compost tea brewer or with equipment you have put together yourself. We have included a design for a five gallon brewer, which is a good size for home gardeners.

Most of the gear for this simple, but effective brewer can be purchased from an aquarium store and a paint store, or online.

Compost tea brewer

- 5 gallon food-grade plastic bucket
- Hydroponic or large aquarium air pump
- 20 feet 3/16" clear vinyl food grade plastic tubing
- Diffusers—aquarium stones or tubing
- Nylon paint strainer bag designed to fit over the top of a five gallon bucket

The air pump plugs into your house current so should **not** be immersed in water. The pump will sit next to the bucket. Each air pump has two or four 3/16" outlets, from which you run 5 foot lengths of the 3/16" tubing into the bottom of the bucket. The ends of the tubing are attached to your diffuser set-up. Air will be pumped into the bottom of the bucket and come out of the diffusers. A compost tea brewer will be more efficient if it utilizes a high volume air pump. Check out hydroponic sources for pumps and diffusers. Also, you can use a lot of creativity in making your diffuser set-ups. A 10 inch circle of ordinary garden soaker hose plumbed down to the 3/16" aquarium hose works well. Some brewers have drilled 1/16" [or smaller] holes in PVC tubing for use as a diffuser. Small fine bubbles are good.

Using your brewer

• Place the diffuser in the bottom of the bucket and connect the tubing to the air pump.

• Fill the bucket almost all the way with water. If you are using municipal water with chlorine , it is important to run the pump for one hour, aerating the water to remove the chlorine.

• Place the clean nylon paint strainer bag into the bucket, securing it with the elastic band around the outside of the bucket top rim.

• Into the open strainer bag carefully place your compost and nutrients, so as not to allow the entire bag to fall into the water.

• Turn on the pump and let it run until the compost tea is brewed—from 24-72 hours.

• Clean all equipment immediately after using it!

Notes:

5 Gallon Compost Tea Brewer

Two 3/16" vinyl tubes go out of the air pump and into the 5 gallon bucket. The white nylon paint strainer bag is secured to the bucket with its own elastic band and hangs inside the bucket. 1 liter of compost will be placed inside the bag after filling the bucket with water.

82

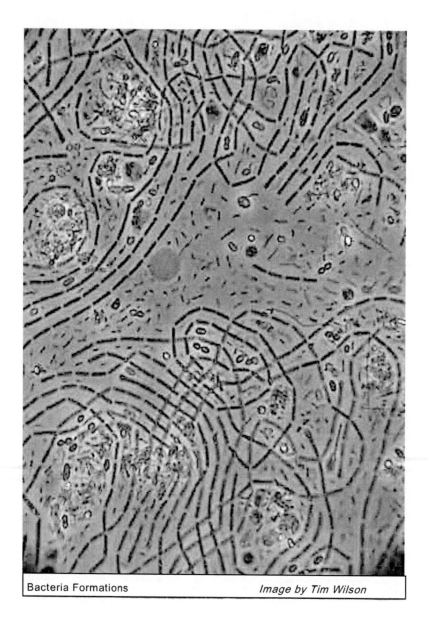

Bacteria Formations   *Image by Tim Wilson*

Biofilm

We presume that in the original *Ghostbusters* movie, the writers choose not to use the technically correct term, "biofilm" simply because it would not read well. Instead they wisely chose the common term, "slime" to create the now infamous statement, "I've been slimed!"

Simply put—slime is biofilm. Bacteria exude a sticky substance which helps them adhere to the walls of arteries, plastic surfaces, stainless steel, or any convenient haven. The sticky compounds that hold biofilm together are made up of carbohydrates called *polysaccharides*.

Mixed with the jelly-like substance may be organic matter from the local environment, such as: pollen, dead skin cells, decaying plant litter, or dead insect parts (to mention a few). All of the extra roughage helps hold the biofilm mass together by strengthening the bond.

Even bacteria of competitive species will huddle together for protection—partners in crime so to speak. Various species of bacteria can typically be identified in a biofilm lab sample.

Studies have shown that pathogens can communicate with each other in the biofilm matrix thanks to a phenomenon called quorum sensing. Somehow, they can perceive how many other bacteria are in close proximity, then react as a group, even if they are of different species. Channels are then created in which nutrients can circulate. Their self created environments effectively become like cities with channels for nutrients to flow in and waste to go out.

The bacteria huddling together in their slime are at least 900 times more resistant to antibiotics and microbicides than they would be as individuals.

Biofilm can be quite difficult to dislodge from it's moorings, requiring mechanical techniques such as pressure washing, vigorous scrubbing, as well as strong chemicals such as 3% hydrogen peroxide solution or chlorine bleach.

Clean your equipment with a 3% peroxide solution, occasionally alternating with a 3% vinegar solution so as not to encourage peroxide resistant bacteria.

There are several reasons why, as compost tea makers we need to be aware of the presence of biofilm. One involves the tendency for biofilm to cling to the compost tea bucket, and all related equipment. The equipment can harbor anaerobic bacteria, therefore needs to be cleaned immediately after every use, leaving no time for the biofilm to harden and become more difficult to remove. Remember, our goal is to keep anaerobic microbes to a minimum in our composting and brewing process.

Biofilm production by bacteria does have it's benefits in the soil. The slime produced by bacteria bind individual soil particles into aggregates, forming larger clumps, causing the soil to have better water retention capacity.

However, during the brewing process we endeavor to gently dislodge the microbes from the soil, flushing them out into the solution, which will encourage them to feed and multiply.

Home brewers can accomplish this by simply stirring vigorously a few times during the brewing process. Large commercial brewing set-ups may have paddles that slowly revolve in the brewing container, encouraging the microbes to break loose. This technique is appropriate for making bacterially dominated teas, but should be performed more sparingly when making a fungal dominated tea because excessive stirring simply breaks up the emerging fungal hyphae strands.

Compost tea recipes for 5 gallons

Basic bacterial compost tea

- Almost 5 gallons of clean chlorine-free water
- 5 cups (1 liter) bacterial compost
- 2 Tablespoons (50 ml.) unsulfured blackstrap molasses
- 2 Tablespoons (50 ml.) soluble cold water kelp
- 1 teaspoon fish hydrolysate (optional)

Basic fungal compost tea

- Almost 5 gallons of clean chlorine-free water
- 1 ½ quarts (1.5 liter) fungal compost
- 2 Tablespoons (50 ml.) humic acid
- 2 Tablespoon (50 ml.) soluble cold water kelp
- 1 Tablespoon (25 ml.) fish hydrolysate
- Extra ingredients: Powdered baby oatmeal, soybean meal, fruit pulp, glacial rock dust, rock phosphate

Basic balanced bacterial/fungal compost tea

- Almost 5 gallons of clean chlorine-free water
- 5 cups (1 liter) bacterial/fungal compost
- 1 Tablespoon (25ml) unsulfured blackstrap molasses
- 1 Tablespoon (25 ml.) humic acid
- 2 Tablespoon (25 ml.) soluble cold water kelp
- 1 teaspoon fish hydrolysate
- Extra ingredients: Powdered baby oatmeal, soybean meal, fruit pulp, glacial rock dust.

Simple Compost Tea

With fewer added nutrients your tea will contain less microbial density, but nevertheless, this recipe can still produce a good, viable tea.

- Almost 5 gallons of chlorine-free water
- 6 cups (1.5 liter) compost or vermicompost
- 3 Tablespoons unsulfured blackstrap molasses

Ingredients

Be careful not to use any additives with microbicides in them. The sulfur in grocery store molasses is an example of a microbial inhibitor. To keep our microbes happy, and encourage vigorous fermentations, we need to go *au-natural* in the fermenter.

Molasses

Unsulfured molasses is the best simple sugar to add for bacteria to feed on. Blackstrap molasses contains a wide range of sugars, and is packed with minerals and nutrients. Molasses also contains humic acid materials, which are beneficial for aerobic fungal growth; but more complex sugars are the preferred food for fungi. Other simple sugars will also work as bacterial foods, such as barley malt or honey. Read the label on the jar of molasses to be certain it does not contain sulfur. Unsulfured molasses can be purchased at health food stores if you cannot find it at your local grocery store. We buy it in bulk at a food co-op, where it is good quality and less than ½ the price. Do not use dry granulated molasses. Dissolve the molasses in a cup of hot water prior to adding it to the fermenter.

Kelp

Kelp provides surface area for fungi to attach to, and has nutrients for both fungi and bacteria. The nutrients that are not consumed by microbes are left for the plants to use.

Cold water kelp is much higher in nutrients than warm water

kelp. *Ascophyllum nodosum* is a commonly available cold-water kelp that can be purchased at garden centers, the Internet, or animal feed stores, where it is sold as powdered algae.

Fungal foods

Fungi feed on slower acting complex sugars provided by oatmeal, soybean meal, corn meal, corn bran, wheat bran, or feather meal. The more finely ground meals are better, which is why powdered baby oatmeal works well (oat flour). Fungi also feed on humic acids.

Fish hydrolysates vs. Fish emulsion

Fish emulsions are what we know of as ordinary "fish fertilizer". They are produced under high heat conditions. The proteins and oils are then separated out and sold as fish meal, and fish oil.

Fish hydrolysates are higher quality products that work as a much better microbial food source. Fish hydrolysates are made using a low heat process known as enzymatic digestion, allowing them to retain their natural oils, amino acids, and nutrients. Companies known to make good quality fish and seaweed products are: Organic Gem and Neptune (USA), and Great Pacific Bioproducts (Canada). There may be others.

Mycorrhizal fungi as a extra bonus additive

Mycorrhizal fungi can be of great benefit to our plants by helping to maintain healthy root systems. However, the heat generated by thermal compost and the conditions in vermicompost are not conducive for the growth of mycorrhizal fungi. If we want mycorrhizal fungi in a batch of compost tea we must add it to the brewer toward the end of the brewing process.

Why? The food resources in a brewing compost tea may cause the mycorrhizal spores to germinate, but if they cannot attach to roots within 24 hours they will die. Therefore, mycorrhizal fungi inoculant is typically added to a finished tea before using it for soil drenching root applications. Dipping seedlings in the fungal tea prior to planting is also of great benefit to young plants. Mycorrihizal fungi inoculant is widely available.

EM® products

EM® stands for "Effective Microorganisms™". EM® is sold as EM•1® in over 100 countries. It consists of a powerful set of unique microbes that can be added to improve the effectiveness, safety, and shelf life of your tea. If you choose to boost the power of your tea, EM•1® should be added after your tea has been fully brewed—prior to application. Please refer to the special chapter on page 107 dedicated to EM®.

Techniques

Brewing a five gallon batch of compost tea is not difficult, requiring very little set-up time, providing the gardener has good compost to work with.

Temperature
Temperature has a direct effect on the total brewing times. We recommend using a digital thermometer for taking the liquid temperature. You will find that you get an accurate reading very quickly. Depending on the quality of the compost, nutrient levels, and aeration factors, typical brewing times are as follows:
- •24 hours @ 75°F. (23°C.)
- •36 hours @ 70°F. (21°C.)
- •42 hours @ 65°F. (18°C.)
- •48 hours @ 60°F. (16°C.)

Please remember that the microbes we are encouraging to grow are a lot like us. They like it room temperature-preferably slightly on the warm side. Does that sound familiar? 72-75°F. (21-23°C) is ideal. Some of the microbes may be very jolly at 85°F. (29°C), but most will slow down dramatically below 68 F.

There is an idea amongst some brewers that the tea should be brewed at the same temperature as the environment it will be applied to. Others consider that a purists attitude. It does remind us of the "proofing" process a winemaker uses to prepare re-hydrated yeast prior to adding it to a fermenter full of grape must. The diligent winemaker avoids shocking the 102°F yeasts by slowly bringing the temperature of the yeast slurry down close to the temperature of the fermenter. This is accomplished by adding some grape juice to it in stages. Using that technique as a caveat, and if the compost tea batch is destined to be diluted with water, cooler ground temperature water can be added to it slowly so as not to shock our microbial guests too much. Some microbes might be tough, and resistant to temperature changes, while others may be quite sensitive.

Compost tea can actually be brewed in the house, as it really does not smell strong, unless it goes anaerobic! If you do brew in the house, please be aware that it can foam out of the brewer at one particular stage, especially when you use vermicompost.

You can start with warm water, by adding some boiled water to the fermenter, bringing it up to about 85°F (29°C). Over the next hour it will cool to 75°F. (24°C), but that will give the microbes a good start. You can buy an aquarium heater, rig up a heating blanket, light bulb, or space heater to keep the fermenter warm, but stable ambient temperature is really the best. Use a thermometer to measure the liquid temperature, as the temperature of your fermenting tea on the floor will probably be several degrees less than what reads on your house thermostat. Simply elevating the bucket could save on energy in your house.

Ultra-violet light

Perhaps we are not as much akin to our microbial friends as we have previously implied, especially for those solar worshipers amongst us. The microbes we use to make compost tea do not like direct UV light, so it is better to situate the fermenter somewhere in the shade or in the dark.

Cover the fermenter?

The brewing compost tea really needs to breath and out-gas, but it can be loosely covered with a board or the plastic lid. We have observed our cat drinking "kitty wine" out of the cup of leachate tea that drips out of our worm bins. There have also been numerous reports of animals, such as dogs—lapping up the brewing compost tea. The "doggy beer" is undeniably nutritious, and is probably not harmful for them, but that has yet to be determined. Considering the disgusting things dogs are eager to eat off of the ground a little compost tea is probably OK. However, if you have animals you may consider covering the bucket. The tea is more valuable than their food. That's what they make dog food for.

Total brewing time

How long it takes for any given batch of compost tea to finish brewing and be ready to use is up for speculation, and depends on many variable factors:

- Quality of compost; How much bacteria and/or fungus
- Nature of compost; Bacterial or fungal?
- Nutrient types
- Amount of nutrients added
- Volume of air injected into the brewer
- Size of air bubbles? (small is good)

•Temperature

•Is the compost in the brewer loose and situated so that the bubbles can pass through it?

The burgeoning compost tea maker must get a feel for their particular environment, situations, compost, and brewer set-up. It is a very good idea to take careful notes, especially concerning nutrients and temperatures.

The brewing equipment we described putting together will usually make a finished bacterial tea in 24-36 hours, and a fungal tea in 24-48 hours.

Troubleshooting

•If you do not add enough nutrients the brewing time will have to be shorter because the microbes will have used up the nutrients. The batch may start to go anaerobic.

•If you add too many nutrients the batch will have a tendency to go anaerobic

•If you brew for too long the nutrients will be used up and the batch may go anaerobic.

•If your brewer is not pumping enough air efficiently into the tea the batch could go anaerobic, especially if there are plenty of nutrients in it. The anaerobic bacteria are always present, and would love to feed on the molasses, kelp etc.. What keeps them at bay is oxygenated conditions they do not care for, and sheer dominance by aerobic microbes.

•A finished tea should look like a brown English ale.

•A finished tea should smell earthy, but NOT stinky. Stench is anaerobic.

•Allow your finished tea to rest for 30 minutes or so, and then use immediately

Evaluating your tea

Ideally, one will use a microscope to check out the microbial growth process. However, there is a simple, practical way to evaluate your compost tea brewing process. A good tea should have a pleasant, clean, but earthy aroma. After making a finished tea, fill a clean drinking bottle half full of your tea, and seal it with a lid. 12 hours later open the bottle and assess it, using your nose. A good smelling tea at that point indicates that you had enough oxygen in your brew. If your tea is stinky, you may need to reduce the level of additives, shorten the brewing time, or lower the temperature in your next batch.

Also consider determining how long it takes for it to become smelly. Aerobic aerated compost teas will all eventually become anaerobic and begin to smell foul. Any given batch of compost tea will peak out after the microbes have consumed the available oxygen and nutrients, and then fall backwards, eventually becoming anaerobic—thus the limited shelf life of our product.

Applications

The first thing to remember about compost tea applications is that you need never worry about applying too much, or too strong a mixture. If in doubt, apply it full strength, and plenty of it. It will not harm the plants.

Soil drenching

For soil drenching, apply to soils that are already wet. The microbes in your fresh compost tea will appreciate being introduced into a similar environment from whence they came. For normal soil drenching maintenance applications dilute 1 part compost tea to 3 parts water (1:3). Soil drenching operations may be performed at any time of day, since UV rays do not penetrate into the soil.

Foliar applications

When using compost tea in foliar applications, make certain all parts of leaf surfaces are covered. To improve adhesion of the tea to leaf surfaces, particularly during moist, cool periods, yucca sap or other natural sticky products can be added. Particulates may need to be filtered out of the tea for use in hand sprayers because of their small spray tips.

Since the microbes in compost tea are sensitive to UV light, it would be prudent to spray before 10:00 AM or after 3:00 PM on sunny days.

For general maintenance foliar applications dilute 1 part compost tea with 1 part water (1:1). However, the general consensus amongst professionals is that if serious pressure from disease is present, the compost tea works best used full strength.

In a situation where known disease problems are present, begin applying tea early in the growing season. When disease pressure is high, apply compost tea once, or even twice per week.

If you are trying to rescue a seriously diseased plant, you can poke holes into the soil in the root zone, and pore compost tea into them, as well as heavy foliar applications with full strength tea.

Orchards

Foliar compost tea applications have shown positive results in the suppression of common diseases in orchards. Strong fungal teas have been shown to control apple scab, cedar apple rust, and scale. Also, it is highly likely that fungal teas will help suppress fireblight in apple orchards.

Fungal teas have also proven their effectiveness in the control of peach leaf curl and peach blossom rot in peach and plum orchards.

Fungal dominated compost teas have also been effective in the control of brown rot in cherry trees. Anthracnose can be suppressed by using a fungal tea for control on the crowns or roots, or a bacterial tea on the leaves. Fusarium may be controlled by using a bacterial dominated compost tea.

It is important when dealing with canopy-related fungal diseases to begin by applying a fungal-dominated soil drench in the fall, so that disease organisms do not have a chance to populate and over-winter in the leaf litter. Apply another soil drench in the spring, and a foliar spray two weeks before bud-break.

Apply compost tea twice per month during the growing season, or once per week if the pressure from disease is high.

Vineyards

Vineyard trials have been fairly extensive, focusing on the control of powdery mildew, downy mildew, and *Botrytis cinerea*. Compost tea applications have shown positive results toward the suppression of crown gall as well.

Strong fungal dominated teas are used both in the soil and on the canopy in vineyards.

Once again, teas applied full strength seem to produce the best results, but for general maintenance the tea may be diluted down to a 1:1 ratio.

It is important when dealing with canopy-related fungal diseases to begin by applying a fungal-dominated soil drench in the fall, so that disease organisms do not have a chance to populate and over-winter in the leaf litter. Apply another soil drench in the spring, and a foliar spray two weeks before bud-break.

50-75 gallons of tea per acre is the typical amount needed for a foliar spray on vineyards with fully developed canopies. Young vineyards with less dense canopies may only require 30-40 gallons per acre to cover all leaf surfaces. During the growing season, vineyards are sprayed twice per month for general maintenance, or once per week if disease pressure is high.

The use of compost teas in vineyards has allowed

viticulturists to reduce their typical copper/sulfur spray applications down to a minimum, sometimes as little as only twice per year.

So far viticulturists have not reported an increase in yields because of the use of compost teas. Lower yields are considered favorable for quality wine grapes.

Lawns

The soils supporting our modern lawns are generally in very poor condition. Already microbially healthy turf will benefit from monthly applications of bacterially dominated compost tea diluted down to 1:4 ratio. Lawns that are in need of rejuvenation will benefit from monthly doses of a balanced fungal/bacterial tea diluted to 1:3. Grasses technically prefer bacterial tea, but if the supporting soil is in poor condition you will need to help it build up a good amount of fungal bio-mass in the first year. If your lawn is well watered prior to applying the compost tea the integration of the microbes into it will be smoother.

Recommended application rates for turf are 20 gallons per acre of compost tea in the autumn. Then beginning in the spring, and extending through the growing season apply 10 gallons per acre per month. That would be 10 gallons of compost tea mixed with 30 or 40 gallons of water per acre per month in the summer.

Gardens

Based on the knowledge we have gleaned from our research, in tandem with our already accumulated gardening experience, we can make specific decisions on how and when to apply compost tea to our garden plants. Some plants, such as asparagus or artichokes, are perennials, so obviously will grow well in soils with plenty of fungal bio-mass. Quick growing annuals, like spinach or lettuce, being nitrogen lovers, will appreciate regular 1:4 doses of bacterial compost tea soil drenches. Fungal problems on your tomato leaves may require full strength foliar applications with a fungal dominated tea, while their root systems will like it if the plants receive regular diluted soil drenches of bacterial teas.

Please remember that soil drenching applications will be more effective if the gardener makes a habit of watering prior to applying compost tea. The microbes in the tea will be more comfortable, and integrate more naturally into a moist environment. Technically, more of the fungal and bacterial biomass survives when the soil is already wet.

A practical approach for many gardeners who are normally busy outside of the garden (at work) would be to ensure that your compost has enough fungal bio-mass in it so that you can create balanced bacterial/fungal teas that will work well in any situation as a general plant tonic.

We all want our gardens to be healthy and beautiful, but not everyone can devote enough time to achieve textbook perfection. Hopefully we are inspired by and find joy in the little miracles that *do* present themselves to us daily in our gardens.

Ordinary gardeners do not need a college education in compost tea to get good results in their home gardens. All well made aerobic compost teas contain both bacteria and fungi, and should give the gardener positive, visible results in a few days. If it takes time to rejuvenate a badly damaged soil environment, please be patient, and don't give up!

Permaculture

What is permaculture? Most home gardeners, upon being presented with that question will stammer. From the gardener's perspective, permaculture may be viewed as some kind of integration between their vegetable garden and the native environment.

The term "permaculture" was actually coined by Australian ecologists in 1978 as an amalgamation of two words: permanent, and agriculture.

It began as a loose idea based on our ethical behavior *towards*, and the integration *with* the natural world. Enthusiasts represent some of the greenest of the green in terms of idealism.

As wonderful as the permaculture movement is, the term is somewhat ambiguous, since it takes the originators of it, and others several paragraphs to define it. This explains why the common gardener may have difficulty waxing eloquently on the subject.

The ideas include design systems for ecologically responsible water-systems, buildings, housing, communities, farming, gardening, plants, animals, soils, waste-water treatment, recycling, and energy use. The list goes on. Even though there may be high-tech gear (like solar panels) utilized, the permaculterist's forte is really in using *low*-tech, and organic systems that integrate so well with each other that they become almost automatic.

So how does one practice permaculture? Something as simple as creating a compost pile instead of stuffing your vegetable waste down the garbage disposal could be considered practicing a permacultural technique. Or, to the other extreme—ones entire property can be re-shaped and designed to incorporate systems endeavoring to be self-sustainable. The ideas can manifest themselves in many forms. If we cannot all commit our life-styles to become full-on card-carrying permaculturists, at least we can integrate some of those ideas and technologies into our own environment.

Without question, compost teas can play an integral role in any permacultural system dealing with plants. In fact, the use of compost teas could be considered quintessential permaculture, because by using them we are encouraging the symbiotic relationships between a multitude of organisms. Symbiosis is an essential element in the permaculture philosophy.

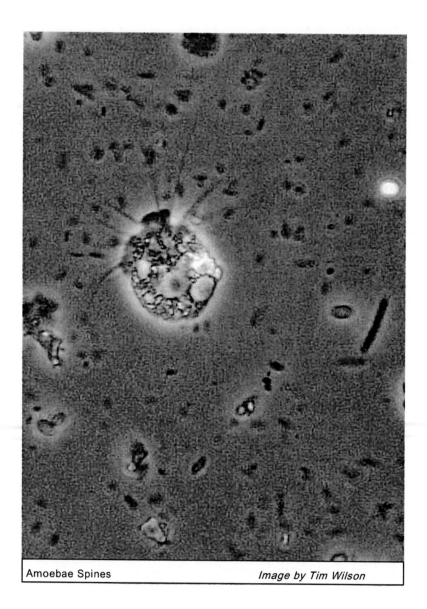

Amoebae Spines   *Image by Tim Wilson*

Interview with Tim Wilson

microbeorganics.com

How did you get into making compost tea?

I have lived on a farm since 1985. We started growing vegetables using conventional methods with fertilizers, and roto-tilling every spring the way they say you are supposed to. Then I started observing the wild plants on the farm, like nettles, yarrow, and mullein. They grew wonderfully without anyone fussing around with them. I began thinking about that and realized that there is something similar to what is taking place in the human gut, where there are microbes that are responsible for breaking down substances. I began doing fermentations with yogurt, fish hydrolysate, worm castings and all kinds of stuff. Finally I discovered Effective Microorganisms (EM), and had some good success with that.

On an EM discussion forum I found out about compost tea, and began building many different types of brewers; venturi types, aquarium pumps with little stones etc.. Finally I came up with the design that I market now. This design uses an air lift. . It produces the greatest amount of dissolved oxygen of any types that I tried. Actually there are two diffusers in the brewer that operate on different principles.

That's a fifty gallon brewer?

Right.

You use a microscope to track what's going on in every batch of compost tea?

The important thing about using a microscope is that you can first evaluate your soil or compost, and see what kind of organisms are in there. You are looking for bacteria, protozoa, and fungal hyphae. Then when you brew your compost tea, it doesn't matter what you do. Every time its going to be slightly different. So the advantage of having a microscope is that you can tell what's going on. Sometimes its going to take 18 hours, or 24 hours, or even 36 hours. It only takes about five minutes to throw it on the slide and see if you have enough bacteria, protozoa or fungi. When you see the microbes you want you stop brewing and use the tea.

What kind of microscope set-up do you use?

I have a Leitz Orthopan epi-fluorescent, phase contrast microscope that was built in the late 1970's. It would be very expensive to buy one of this quality now. I have a Sony high definition camcorder hooked up to it with a computer interface so I can watch the microbes moving around and record directly to the hard drive. You don't have to have a camera hooked up to it like I do, but the ones I sell both have camera ports.

What are they like?

One is an inexpensive monocular type that works just fine, and the other is a bigger trinocular model. They are made in China. I searched for a long time to find microscopes that were of the quality I wanted with metal and brass gears, but still at a good price. I also had the company make 20X objectives for them, because that is a really important size for viewing some of these microbes. Modern microscopes usually only come with 10X, 40X, and 100X objectives.

You created a special filter for viewing the microbes in compost tea?

Yes. I spent a lot of time on that. By trial and error, I tested hundreds of different filter samples, using advice from some of the best microscopists. I was looking for a particular type of enhancement which created a 3D or phase contrast effect. After two months of working on it every day I was still not satisfied. One day I was sitting there, and the thought came to me that I should try exactly what the experts said you should not do—and that worked.

Wow, that's the kind of contrarian science I like!

Well it worked, and those are the filters I offer with the microscopes, along with an instructional DVD set, that teaches how to deal with the microscope, examine soil and compost as well as prepare slides. I sell an additional DVD set which instructs how to identify soil, compost and compost tea microorganisms.

What is the kind of microbial activity you are looking for in compost tea?

Well, the plant puts out carbon molecules through its root system that feeds bacteria. That, in turn triggers the population of protozoa; and usually what we are looking at is flagellates and naked amoeba that hatch out, or excyst which is the technical term. They come out of the cysts they have been waiting in. The protozoa multiply, and eat the bacteria. The protozoa only utilize from 30-40% of the food, leaving 60-70% that is expelled from them and becomes bio-available nutrients for the plant.

That's one system. Another involves mycorrhizal fungi which directly feeds the roots of the plant. Simplistically, if you were going to split it in two you would say that the action that occurs between the protozoa and the bacteria provides nitrogen, and the action that occurs with the mycorrhizal fungi provides phosphorus and potassium. But it is not really that cut and dry as mycorrhizae provide nitrogen in many plants and so on. It's really more complicated than that.

There is a lot more going on in there. There is also the activity of other species of fungi. In compost tea mycorrhizal fungi does not grow well. What does usually grow is called fungi imperfecti—which is fungi that grows without a fruiting body. Fungi contributes to the structure of the soil, and is a food source for bacteria. Usually you will want to see bacteria, protozoa and fungi in a finished compost tea.

The nematodes do not really populate well in compost tea?

No, they have a complex system of propagating that involves laying eggs that hatch out. I have seen a lot of them drown in compost tea.

You have used Canadian peat moss as an inoculant for compost tea?

Yes. There are the stories that have gone around that sphagnum peat mosses are inert, but I have found that to be simply not true. I bought some to check it out, and found bacteria, protozoa, and fungal hyphae as well coming out in the sample. I tried several different bags and noticed that the microbial content varies from bag to bag. In every one there were some sort of beneficial microbes. So I often throw in a handful of sphagnum peat moss when I start a batch of compost tea.

You have used forest soil as an inoculate as well?

Well, with forest soil or with grassland soil—if you are growing a certain type of plant it could be beneficial to inoculate it with soil you can get from an area where a similar type of plant is growing healthy in the wild.

Because of all of the scuttle on the internet about the damage pumps can do to compost tea you did some experiments. Can you tell us about that?

After I read that impeller-type pumps tear up the organisms—in particular fungal hyphae—I decided to check it out. We ran several tests where we put our compost tea through various pumps and nozzle types. We looked at that and found that the organisms survived just fine, with about 5-10% damage at the most. However, I would assume that if you were recirculating the tea through a pump over and over, like to make compost tea, it may cause damage. Surprisingly we tested spraying the tea through some of those little plastic household-type squeeze sprayers and found that the damage was very severe. We recommend people use regular pump-up type garden sprayers.

You have a farm. What is your experience with the effectiveness of compost teas?

By the time we started making compost tea, we had already switched over to mostly organic growing techniques, but we were still having problems with powdery mildew in our greenhouse. We began spraying it through our overhead sprinklers in a very fine mist, which not only wet the leaves but soaked into the soil as well. Eventually the mildew virtually disappeared. We must, however, remember that compost tea is not miracle cure, a magic bullet that will just fix anything.

Who do you know that is using compost tea commercially?

I have sold quite a few set-ups to lawn-care companies, particularly in the USA on the east coast. They are doing quite well, particularly the ones that also got microscopes. It has been fulfilling for me to get feedback from some of them as to how well it is working for them. That's what is kind of the motivating thing for me is to try to bring about what little change I can from my small corner of the world.

I see compost tea as a fledgling movement, really still in it's infancy.

I would like to tell you about a fellow I know that has about a one acre greenhouse that he uses for commercial cut-flowers. He ended up with an erwinia infection, which is a pathogenic bacteria toxic to plants. He was growing really rare cala lilies, hydrangeas, and other plants. He was devastated, and went to the local government agriculture office, and they said he was hooped and that he would have to remove everything, including the soil, from the greenhouse and start over. He had some rare bulbs he had suitcased in from Portugal. So he did some reading— Elaine Ingham— on compost tea and he decided he was going to do that. He eventually made himself a brewer out of a freestanding swimming pool, and just kept applying it over and over. All the other commercial growers just laughed at him as he persisted. He couldn't see anything happening. He just kept at it for about 4--6 months until he started seeing it work. It just transformed his whole operation.

He started getting higher yields, and the best looking flowers that he had ever had. He applied the tea straight, you know, undiluted. I have known him for about eight years, and he retired last year, but it was his ninth year of growing that way. What is interesting is that in the last two years he didn't use compost tea at all because the microbes had established themselves so well in the soil that all he had to do was a little top dressing with compost and that was it.

Wow, that's good to know

Yea, and what's more he just grows the hydrangeas and cuts the flowers off and then when they die back in the fall it seems that almost as soon as the leaves hit the ground they are consumed by microbes.

That's an amazing testimonial

Well it sure convinced me

Thanks for all of the information, and taking the time to share what you have experienced.

No problem

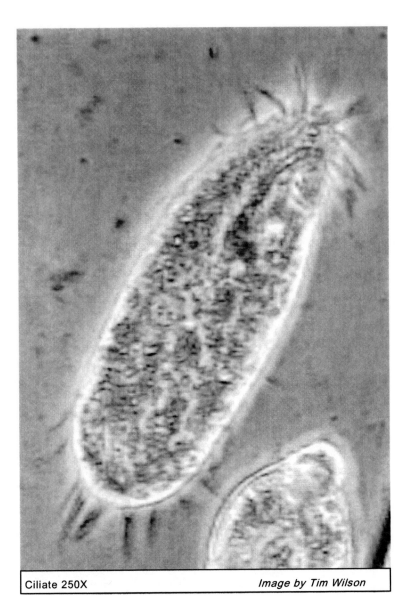

Ciliate 250X   *Image by Tim Wilson*

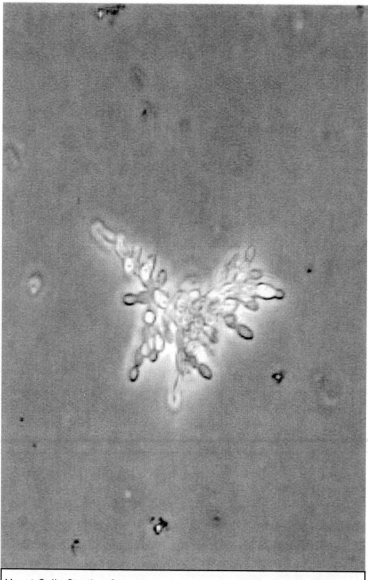

Yeast Cells Starting Structure   *Image by Tim Wilson*

EM•1®

In 1980, Dr. Teruo Higa, Professor of Horticulture at the University of Ryukyus, Japan began experimenting with microbes deemed beneficial for soil and plant health. What he found was a specific group of microbes that work very well as a team. These super-athletes are actually common microbes: lactic acid bacteria, phototrophic bacteria, particular strains of yeasts, fermentative fungi, and actimomycetes.

The EM•1® set of organisms do a great job out-competing pathogens, and exhibit an amazing ability to degrade dioxins and many other pollutants. Because of that, EM•1® products have a wide range of applications, beyond what is covered in this text.

Here we are concerned with only our specific horticultural uses, as EM•1® microorganisms work in similar fashion, and in tandem with our beneficial aerobic compost tea microbes already described here.

Some of the organisms in EM•1® are actually faculative **anaerobic** microorganisms, which can exist in both low oxygen and high oxygen environments. The product contains aerobic microbes as well. **Hopefully this will not be confusing to the reader!** Up until this point, we have been promoting only the growth of **aerobic** microbes in our teas, the reasons for which we hope have been made clear. We are not suggesting opening the door to all anaerobic organisms, but a specific set that can be used in a controlled fashion.

We shall lapse once again into our dinner party analogy.

As the producers of this event, we may choose to invite guests to our microbial dinner party who speak a foreign language, and bring their own customs with them. As a concerned host we must be confident that our foreign guests will enjoy the fare presented at the table, and in turn contribute in their own unique way, yielding a memorable experience for all. We are after all, an international community, honoring the best other cultures have to offer.

The combination of aerobic compost tea and EM•1® has yielded excellent results as attested to by recent testimonials, and is a practical study in progress.

Several companies market products containing various combinations of beneficial microorganisms, but we are recommending the original EM® products based on the work of Dr. Higa, which use his specific formulation of microbes.

We are offering our website compostteamaking.com as a forum for further discussions, specific recommended doses, application rates, and links to EM•1® products.

Using EM•1® in combination with compost tea

After your compost tea batch has been fully brewed, you may add the EM•1® product to it prior to applying the tea. The combined products are highly recommended, and will add a bit more shelf life to it than plain compost tea. Apply the combined product within 24 hours after the brewing process has been completed.

Benefits of EM•1® in compost tea

•Contains large populations of beneficial microbes, enzymes, trace minerals, vitamins, and organic acids, adding to the microbial complexity of compost tea.

•Kills pathogens that may be errant in compost tea

•Helps increases the shelf-life of aerobic compost tea—from hours to days

•Encourages the growth of mychorrizae, fungi, and worms

•Improves the over-all effectiveness of aerated compost teas

Bokashi

"Bokashi" means "fermented product" in the Japanese language. The method is a popular technique for composting kitchen scraps using EM•1® or various other microbes, the primary being lactic acid producing bacteria.

Traditionally, the technique was used in Japan by fermenting rice hulls in warm water, then using the liquid as a compost starter. The kitchen scraps became broken down by a kind of pickling process induced by the lactic acid bacteria in the rice.

Today, simple cultures capable of composting in a similar way can be made using yogurt, which also contains plenty of *lactobacillus* bacteria

The modern EM•1® microbe teams will do a much more efficient job of composting than a simple mono-culture like *lactobacillus*. EM•1® is a unique blend of proprietory anaerobic lactic acid-producing bacteria, specific yeasts, and phototropic bacteria.

After purchasing EM•1® , enthusiasts can maintain a per-petual supply of EM•1® by culturing it in the form of bokashi. The completed bokashi itself can be used as a starter to make more. However, it may be wise to occasionally purchase fresh EM•1® to ensure that the microbes do not mutate or are infected by less functional microbes. If, and how much mutation or infection may occur is up for specula-tion Actually, studies have shown EM•1® microbes to be very persistent, durable, and have a strong tendency to remain stable in many diverse conditions.

Adding bokashi to a batch of compost tea after the tea has been fully fermented is the same as adding EM•1®, except obviously the bokashi must be rendered into a liquid prior to adding it to the blend. (see below)

Bokashi Recipe

- 50 pounds rice bran or wheat bran
- 3.5 gallons water
- 1.5 cups of EM•1®
- 1.5 cups of molasses

Procedure

- Boil 1 gallon of the water, and mix the molasses into it
- Combine the molasses water with the other 2.5 gallons of water
- The temperature should be between 90-105°F. (32-41°C)
- Add the 1.5 cups EM•1® to the water solution
- Mix the water/molasses solution slowly into the bran
- Put the mixture into an airtight container
- Maintain temperature above 70°F. (21°C) 80-100 F. is better
- Depending on the temp., it will take 1-4 weeks to ferment
- Finished bokashi will smell like pickles, but faintly pleasing
- White mold (yeast) growing on top is OK. Green or black mold is not OK

Bokashi can be stored at room temperature-sealed for up to a year, or it can be dried at up to 200 degrees F. (max.) (94°C), vacuum packed, and stored for longer periods.

Activating bokashi and rendering it into a liquid

- Put 2 cups of bokashi into a gallon container
- Boil 2 cups of water and mix 1 teaspoon of molasses into solution
- Fill the container with water and the molasses solution
- Put the lid on the container
- Keep the container at 75°F. (24°C) for one to two weeks

The reader may have noticed that these formulas did not call for *un-sulfured* molasses. Why? Because the EM•1® organisms have no problem digesting a little sulfur. If they can digest toxins, petroleum, dye residue, heavy metals and dioxins, dealing with some sulfur is child's-play for these microbial super-heroes. However, we still recommend buying your molasses at a food co-op or similar source based solely on the price. Grocery store molasses is an extremely overpriced product considering that molasses (wholesale) is one of the cheapest sugars used in the food industry.

Using bokashi for composting kitchen scraps

The bokashi method of dealing with kitchen scraps involves layering the bokashi, scraps, and newspaper in successive 2" layers. Bokashi can break down meat, fat, and bones as well as vegetables and grains, but one needs to add more bokashi when composting meat scraps. The total amount of bokashi should be about 15% of what is in the bucket.

Begin by putting a layer of bokashi in the bottom of the bucket. Add some kitchen scraps on top of the bokashi, and finally a layer of shredded newspaper. The newspaper will help inhibit oxygen, retain moisture, and provides a carbon source for the microbes. Press the layer down to keep air out, put an airtight lid on the bucket and keep it warm.

Continue layering more bokashi, scraps and paper until the contents of the bucket can be transferred to another larger container to complete the fermentation. Any thing you can do to keep the temperature in the buckets between 75 – 90 degrees F. will speed up the process. In ideal situations, the bokashi method can yield usable compost in as little as ten weeks.

When putting the bokashi into your garden its important to note that animals like to eat bokashi, as it is good for their intestinal tracts.

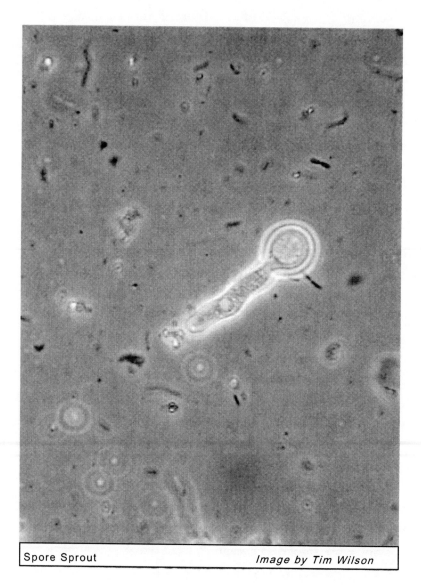

Spore Sprout   *Image by Tim Wilson*

CONCLUSION

P lease do not be discouraged if the creation of compost tea seems difficult. Once you get your system down, and are familiar with your own particular parameters we are confident that you will find compost teas quite easy to make.

Also, like myself, once you begin to observe the benefits compost teas are giving to your plants you may unwittingly become part of our earthy crusade, spreading the good word—or at least find yourself sympathetic to it. Healthier soils will help everyone world-wide. With the technology we now have at our fingertips, a strong scientific backbone, and wisdom accumulated through the ages we possess the keys to a responsible stewardship capable of making our agricultural world into a paradise.

Older agricultural-based economic systems have been pushed aside with disdain like yesterdays coffee by many modern-day economists. Perhaps there are those that need to be reminded where all of our food comes from. Natural resources and agriculture represent the residual wealth of most durable economically powerful nations. Whenever I fly from coast to coast on a clear day over the USA, I am always amazed at how much cultivated land there is between the Atlantic and Pacific Oceans. From the air Europe is a stunning magic green carpet of small farms and vineyards. I have yet to fly over China.

It is typical for the organic-leaning garden contingent (like myself) to rag about the evils of conventional agricultural practices. It's easy and convenient to do so while reclining in comfortable chairs in our home offices. Perhaps it is just a little too easy for us to judge what others do or do not do. Statistically, most buyers of certified organic produce live near urban centers where practically no agriculture takes place.

Depending on the crop, one farmer with good equipment can manage hundreds of acres. We have mentioned that over-tillage can harm the fungi present in the soil, but a tiller is an excellent method for weed control. No one wants to weed hundreds of acres by hand. Permaculture activists would suggest that it can be done on a smaller scale, but do we really want to go back to small subsistence farming? Not everyone wants to grow *all* of their own food. I may know a few things about growing fruit and vegetables in a home environment, but admit to having little knowledge of producing them on a larger scale.

Therefore, I tip my hat to the ranchers and farmers of our planet, who work hard to feed us all. Yes, there are certainly many improvements yet to be made in worldwide agricultural techniques, but I honor those that are actually doing it-producing food-and lots of it. Volume is good, because there are still over one billion hungry people in our world.

For many years I bought my annual potatoes from a small 80 acre local farm. The farmers grew potatoes in their field of gorgeous Mt. Rainier glacial silt, with no additives, no fertilizers, no chemicals, and no water! One hot, late-August day I asked "John" the younger farmer how they went about irrigating all of those potatoes. He looked at me like I was crazy. "We don't put no WATER on 'em", he said. OK. They were very common people, and did not charge enough for their produce. If asked whether they were using organic methods on their farm they would look at you cross-eyed. Were their potatoes organic? No. Were the potatoes good? Yes! I went back every year.

During harvest season I will make U-turns to visit gardeners and small farmers produce stands. The ultimate pleasure is unquestionably the leave-your-money-in-the-cup experience. Yes folks! There still are some rare places in America where we are privileged to be honored with that kindly trust. Just drop your coins into the dirty little poke-mon cup, grab your zucchini and cucumbers and go. It doesn't get any better.

Woe to he who would breach that simple trust

But not I
I am a cup that is filled with the most delicate of wines
A sun that shines on the noble of heart
A child who peers with wonder into the cauldron of knowledge
A tiny glimmer of sunlight tenuously falling into a mossy glen
A salmon who struggles up-stream to finally leave her eggs
A mighty ancient tree who has no concept of death
A sun spewing out an unimaginable abundance of energy
A galaxy speckled with quiet blinking stars
A universe filled with the void

It is our destiny to experience realities greater than we do today

Please visit us at
www.compostteamaking.com

References

Appelhof, Mary, *Worms Eat My Garbage*. 2nd ed. Flowerfield Press 1997

Barnes, Robert D., *Invertebrate Zoology*. 2nd ed. Saunders Co. 1968

Clarke O., *Oz Clarkes Encyclopedia of Grapes*. Websters International 2001

Higa, T., *Our Future Reborn-EM Technology Changes the World*. Sunmark, Tokyo 2006

Ingham, E., *The Compost Tea Brewing Manual*. Soil Food Web Inc. Corvallis, Oregon

Ingham, E., *The Field Guide to Actively Aerated Compost Tea*. Soil Food Web Inc. Corvallis, Oregon

Johnson, H., *The Story of Wine*. Mitchell Beazley, London 1989

Johnson, H., J. Robinson, *The World Atlas of Wine*. Mitchel Beazley, London 2001

Lowenfels, J., W. Lewis, *Teaming with Microbes*. Timber Press Inc. 2006

Nancarrow, L., J.H. Taylor, *The Worm Book*. Ten Speed Press, Berkeley 1998

Norman, R., *Rhone Renaissance*. Wine Appreciation Guild 1996

Proal, A., *Understanding Biofilms*. Bacteriality Publications May 26th, 2008

Rombaugh, L., *The Grape Grower-A Guide to Organic Viticulture*. Chelsea Green 2002

Wilson, T., *Organic Growing From a Microbial Perspective*. Microbeorganics.com

Resources

Compost Tea Forum
compostteamaking.com

Compost Tea
www.simplici-tea.com
www.organicapproach.com

Compost
www.jgpress.com
www.alaskahumus.com
www.organicgem.com
www.greatwesternsales.com
www.greatpacificbioproducts.com (Canada)

Worms
www.yelmworms.com (USA)
www.wormswrangler.com (USA)
www.wormtec.com.au (Australia)

Fungi
www.mycorrhizae.com
www.fungi.com
www.tandjenterprises.com

Hardware
www.microbeorganics.com
www.milescoscientific.com
www.professionalmicroscopes.com
www.hydroponics.com

Index

CPSIA information can be obtained
at www.ICGtesting.com
Printed in the USA
LVOW12s0027181017
552826LV00001B/169/P